Robert M. Gooch
Troy, Virginia 22974

The
Dove Shooter's
Handbook

The
Dove Shooter's
Handbook

Dan M. Russell

Winchester Press

Copyright © 1974 by Dan M. Russell
All rights reserved

Library of Congress Catalog Card Number: 73-88878
ISBN: 0-87691-135-1

First printing June 1974
Second printing September 1974

Published by Winchester Press
460 Park Avenue, New York 10022

PRINTED IN THE UNITED STATES OF AMERICA

*This book
is dedicated to the
dove hunter*

Picture Credits

Photographs in this book are by the author and the following contributors, listed alphabetically.

Frank Collins: page 49.

Byron W. Dalrymple: pages 16, 27, 28-29, 32, 45, 90, 95, 137, 143, 150, 197.

Jack Dermid, North Carolina Wildlife Resources Commission: page 60.

Fred Hardy: pages 87, 210, 211.

Carl Kays: pages 44, 67, 115, 124, 198.

Lee Nelson: pages 83, 122, 207.

Leonard Lee Rue III: pages 34, 38, 54, 56 (top and bottom), 57 (top and bottom), 58 (top and bottom), 76.

Tennessee Game & Fish Commission: pages 30, 113 (top), 203.

Russell Tinsley: pages 22-23, 24, 104, 106, 107, 109, 111, 112, 117, 121, 127, 131, 141, 154, 172, 226, 236.

U.S. Fish & Wildlife Service: page 19.

Acknowledgments

No matter how much I might say here, it would be inadequate to thank all of those who helped me with this book. Generally speaking, everyone listed in the bibliography—in fact, everyone who has done any work with doves—contributed in some measure. I am especially indebted to the personnel of the Kentucky Department of Fish and Wildlife Resources for their assistance during all the years of the dove study; to my colleagues in the Southeastern states with whom I worked on projects and committees involving dove management, and to persons in other regions conducting similar projects; to the U.S. Fish and Wildlife Service personnel in the Migratory Birds Population Station, the Disease Laboratory, and the Branch of Game Management who have worked along with the states and regions to solve area-wide problems in dove management. I would like to pay special tribute to Frank Winston of the Florida Game and Fresh-Water Fish Commission, who directed the Southeastern States Dove Studies during a crucial time, and to James Keeler of the Alabama Department of Conservation, who is currently leading the dove-study efforts in the Southeast. And I want to thank my wife, Vivian, for her great aid in cataloging, filing and typing.

Contents

Introduction 10

1. *The Game and the Shooter 16*
2. *Life History of the Dove 32*
3. *Dove Shooting 94*
4. *Doves on the Table 136*
5. *Regulations and Harvest . . . and the Importance of Hunting 150*
6. *Dove Management 178*
7. *Questions and Prospects 226*

   Selected Bibliography of Dove Literature 237

   Index 251

Introduction

Many times while working dove shoots or on other dove-study assignments, I've been asked questions about some aspect of a dove's make-up or life history. When there was no obvious or sure answer, I tried to come up with a reasonable answer. Consequently, over the years I developed a whole sackful of reasonable answers. It was something of a surprise at first to find so much interest among the dove hunters in something other than just shooting. But they do want to know about their doves, and that's a fact. It is commonly known among men in the field (but seldom discussed) that hunters develop a special regard for their quarry, particularly for the welfare and protection of the game. I won't attempt to explain this reverence, but any hunter will know it's true.

As years went by it became more and more obvious that there was a need for a book that answered hunters' questions about doves, if for no other reason than to satisfy that special regard. And of course, the more the hunter knows, the more enjoyment he gets from the sport, and the better it is for the doves.

This book contains an index to simplify looking things up, for I hope that after you've read the book through you will keep it around for reference when a question comes up. It is somewhat brief, but as some sage once suggested, "anyone can write a long book, but it takes real work to boil out the non-essentials." With a concise reference you might spend less time finding your answer; you might also have to figure some things out for yourself. For your information, pleasure and further reading, I have added a bibliography of selected dove literature as an appendix to this book. Though it is far from complete, enough has been included to show the many phases of dove study and the wide and varied interest in doves.

You might like to know how all this information on doves was developed. The earliest work on doves (and many other species) was done by private individuals — people simply interested in birds, as some people are interested in baseball or growing rare plants. Some of these early workers very meticulously wrote up their observations in such publications as *The Wilson Bulletin, The Auk, Condor* and others. These numerous writings became our early records and the foundation for detailed studies by professional workers later on.

Among the earlier professionals working on doves were H. Elliot McClure, in Iowa, and George C. Moore, in Alabama. Both of these men did their work in the early 1940's as students in professional training. The results of their studies provided a platform for present-day management. McClure's work on cooing doves tied in with present-day call-count censuses. Moore's early work on life history and production stands as an example in wildlife research. However, both of these men at that time viewed the dove only as a bird in need of protection, not as an annual renewable resource that ought to be utilized. In fact, most early studies were protection-oriented. So were the hunting regulations, and a strictly protective attitude reigned at meetings to formulate regulations.

In late 1948 and 1949 the U.S. Fish and Wildlife Service, the Southeastern states and the Wildlife Management Institute combined efforts and organized the Southeastern Cooperative Dove Research Project. The accomplishments of this joint undertaking are widely known. During and since that time, numerous professionals have worked with doves or studied some special, hidden facet in their life history or management; the resulting accumulation of knowledge is enormous. I think all people involved today in the management of doves would agree that the major influence—the beginning of our modern dove-management program—was the dedicated work of George C. Moore in adapting realistic goals and policies regarding protection, utilization and management.

When I talk about doves I usually have mourning doves in mind. They are distributed throughout the U.S., can presently be hunted in 31 of the mainland states plus Hawaii, and are far more abundant than any of the related species on this continent (unless you count the common domestic pigeon, sometimes called the rock dove, which belongs to the same family). In terms of hunting, the mourning dove is far more important nationally than any of its relatives, and therefore this book is primarily concerned with the mourning dove. Moreover, my own experience as a wildlife biologist studying doves has been almost entirely in the Southeast, where the mourning dove reigns supreme.

All the same, other species are hunted in certain regions. Of these species, the best-known is the white-winged dove, which is currently hunted in Arizona, California, Nevada, New Mexico and Texas. The whitewing is highly prized in its area and it has been the subject of considerable study and writing. For a bird of limited distribution, it causes a lot of commotion — especially when you consider that the hunting period is brief. As in the case of the mourning dove, states set their whitewing seasons within a federal framework, but that framework usually allows for a season that lasts a month or less, a much shorter period than we have for mourning doves. The shooting usually opens September 1 and is mostly ended by September 30, though in some of the lower parts of the range the season is later because the migrating birds arrive later. The hunter's harvest of whitewings is carefully controlled, with shooting regulated by counties and zones. Sometimes whitewings are hunted along with mourning doves, as they're likely to occupy pretty much the same areas, and a large number of Western hunters shoot whitewings exclusively or in excess of mourning doves. Generally speaking, aside from having adapted to arid country and relying more heavily on weed fields and wild foods in ranch country, whitewings aren't all that different from mourning doves. However, since they are popular—even if they're only hunted in five states rather than 31—I won't ignore them. Where differences between the species deserve to be mentioned I'll do so, and I'll include tips from very experienced whitewing hunters.

The other related species are so limited in distribution that they account for a very small portion of the shooting. In Puerto Rico, for example, you may hunt the scaly-naped pigeon, the white-crowned pigeon and the Zenaida dove as well as the mourning dove and a subspecies of the whitewing. And, by special permit, the band-tailed pigeon may be hunted in the mountain valleys of California, Washington, Oregon, Arizona, New Mexico, Utah and Colorado. If you live in one of the places I mentioned or plan an autumn trip there, you may want to pick up a copy of the federal regulations at your post office and plan to put a little extra variety into your hunting. It's necessary to be familiar with those regulations in any event—plus the game laws of the state you hunt in—regardless of which species you hunt.

But no more needs to be said here about the less important members of the dove family. What I want to do is share with you my knowledge and the knowledge of others regarding the most important members of that family, the birds that contribute most to our wingshooting sport.

1
The Game and The Shooter

The mourning dove has a lilting, exotic-sounding scientific name: *Zenaidura macroura macroura*. The Eastern race is *Zenaidura macroura carolinensis* and the Western race is *Zenaidura macroura marginella*. The first part of these Latin designations has a romantic origin that few dove shooters know about. Prince Charles Lucien Bonaparte (1803–1857), a nephew of Napoleon, devoted most of his life to ornithological and zoological science instead of political conquest. At the age of 22 he began publication of a major four-volume work, *American Ornithology*, in which he named and described a number of birds—including doves, of course. Bonaparte's wife was named Zénaïde. Thus we have a number of doves whose scientific names begin with *Zenaida* or *Zenaidura*. (And a tropical variety, legally hunted in Puerto Rico, is known in English as the Zenaida dove.) The sec-

Devoted dove shooter enjoys experimenting. Decoys are effective and popular; calls are less so.

ond part of the mourning dove's scientific name—*macroura*—describes the bird's long tail, and the third term has to do with where each race is (or was) located.

The dove is a member of the pigeon family *Columbidae*. As books tell it, there are about 500 species and subspecies of this pigeon family over the globe, about 100 of which are found in America, but only 17 or so range north of the Mexican border. The most common are the rock dove, or domestic pigeon, the mourning dove and the white-winged dove (*Zenaida asiatica*), commonly called whitewing for short. The whitewing is found in the Southwestern U.S. and is hunted along with the mourning dove in that region.

A great deal has been written about the pheasant, the grouse, the Canada goose and other fine game species. By comparison, the dove has been neglected; but practically any way you look at it, the dove is the most important game bird in the country. It ranges over the entire United States, from Canada to Mexico and points south, and from sea level to elevations of some 10,000 feet up in the mountains. This highly mobile bird has readily adapted, even prospered, with the changes in our agriculture, economy and increased hunting pressure. The dove qualifies as the "now" bird, fulfilling our present-day demands for hunt-

Most common American dove species is mourning dove. This one is mature male, weighing about five ounces.

ing recreation while most other species, including waterfowl, pheasants, quail and such require careful husbandry to maintain usable population levels. It seems strange that so little has been written about the dove for the dove hunter.

Everyone has an opinion about mourning doves. As Frederick C. Lincoln pointed out in a U.S. Fish and Wildlife Service Bulletin he prepared in 1945: "Few birds exert a stronger esthetic and sporting appeal than does the mourning dove.

The trim beauty of its form, the soft delicate shades of color touched by spots of metallic luster, the whistling sound emitted by the rapid beat of wings in a swift, arrowlike flight that calls for the greatest skill of the marksman, and the soothing plaintive quality of its call-notes make it popular with both sportsmen and nature students."

Although it is estimated that perhaps about half of the annual dove mortality is due to hunting, only three out of ten doves are lucky enough to live out their first year. Whether hunted or not, the population turnover is between 65 and 80 percent each year. One in a hundred might reach the extremely old age of six or eight years in the wild. Once I retrapped one eight years after I had banded it, but that was very unusual. If there are records of older doves, they are very few.

Given 30 doves at nesting time, their numbers will climb to 100 by the end of summer. Then they will just as surely be back to 30 at the start of the next nesting season. This is the law of nature: Animals having a high reproductive rate must of necessity be short-lived. Otherwise, we'd be up to here in doves.

Land-use changes seem to have been beneficial to doves, especially in hunting states where they apparently have become more adaptable, hardier, better able to take advantage of larger grain fields and increased grain production. We have experienced an increase of dove hunters, increased bag limits and total harvest—evidently along with an increased dove population. (If this is not so—if the dove population has always been as large as it is today—then we have allowed a pitifully small hunting harvest in past years.) How far this can go is a matter of conjecture, but it does appear that you can have your doves and shoot them, too. By taking proper precautions to safeguard the broodstock, by keeping tabs on population levels and by controlling the kill through prudent regulation of hunting, we should be able to perpetuate doves for hunting throughout the foreseeable future.

Projecting from present estimates, we can predict fielding some two to 2½ million dove shooters per season, and they may harvest 40 to 50 million doves annually. Dove hunts could add up to 12 to 15 million recreation days each year. The economic impact of all this is—to put it mildly—fantastic.

Most sportsmen seem to share a few common traits—an interest in the ways of game; a day-to-day optimism about finding game, shooting well and filling the bag; a willingness to support wildlife management. But there may be no "typical" dove hunter any more than there's a typical pheasant hunter or a typical sheep hunter. The dove

Southeastern shooter stays low and waits patiently in

hunter is really a shooter and a dove hunt is really a dove shoot. There isn't much actual *hunting* for doves. The hunting is a matter of first locating a flock. From there on it is dove shooting.

The dove shooter, whatever else he may be, is not a "meat hunter." In fact, the cost of this sport in terms of meat on the table makes for ridiculously extravagant eating. I watched a young shooter once, popping away at every dove he could see. I

feeding field where flights will provide pass shooting.

asked him if he had any idea how many caps he'd busted so far.

"Well, that's not hard to figure, just count the empty boxes."

I did, and there were four, plus half of the one he was then working on.

"But I got eight doves!"

"Not too bad," I said. "Just a shade over half a box of shells per dove. If you load your own you

Thoughtful gunner saves spent shells for reloading and avoids littering farmer's field with his hulls.

may be getting by for less than a dollar a bird."

"Huh? Oh—wow! Don't tell my wife. Just don't tell my wife."

I didn't even know his wife, but I can easily imagine her reaction if someone had told her about the cost of dining on doves. Chances are, a lot of you know how expensive it can be.

Dove shooting does attract the affluent (and these days that includes just about everyone from the schoolboy to the industrial magnate). Short work hours, daylight-saving time, four-day-week, half a day off on Wednesdays—all these factors contribute to the dove-shooting syndrome. The dove shooter is usually a pretty good sport, too. I want to splice in a compliment here: He is one sportsman, for certain, who pays in taxes and license fees to perpetuate his game. We know his group has contributed millions of dollars to research and management and because of this the dove is better assured a permanent place in our dynamic society than is the bluebird, robin, thrush or other non-hunted species. And, among all hunters, the dove shooter contributes the greater share, proportionately, to the Federal Aid to Wildlife Restoration Fund. This is simply because he does so much more shooting.

Let me quote statements by the Wildlife Management Institute in April and May, 1972, issues of the *Outdoor News Bulletin:* "After all the concern and talk during 1971 about imminent dangers to wildlife, official tallies show that American sportsmen were the ones who provided most of the money for the improvement of wildlife resources last year. . . . Although bombarded by unknowing protectionists who contributed virtually nothing toward assisting wildlife, sportsmen supported wildlife protection and management efforts to the tune of over $256 million . . . for licenses, tags, permits and stamps. These revenues are used by states to protect and manage all wildlife and fish resources, including endangered species, not just game animals. . . . An additional $47.8 million was made available to wildlife agencies through the Federal Aid to Fish and Wildlife Restoration Programs. These monies come from manufacturers' excise taxes on sporting arms and ammunition. . . ."

And then, in reporting on the President's signing of the proclamation designating September 23, 1972, as National Hunting and Fishing Day, the *Bulletin* quoted the Presidential observation that "for many years, responsible hunters and fishermen have been in the vanguard of efforts to halt the destruction of our land and waters and protect the natural habitat so vital to our wildlife." He went on to recognize sportsmen for promoting recreational outlets for sportsmen and non-sportsmen

Flock of whitewings leaves roosting area to feed; this is one wave of flight that lasted two hours.

In southern Arizona's cholla-cactus country, hunter ma

alike. He also recognized the sportsmen's enormous monetary contributions, which constitute most of the funds used to protect and enhance the nation's wildlife resources.

The President could have added that it is most often the hunter who leads the conservation movements because he has first-hand knowledge of the needs of the wildlife species. The hunter is interested, so he becomes better informed than most people. He is often the guy who gets up in

et high shots at either mourning doves or whitewings.

arms against the devastating stream-channelization projects, and who advocates farming practices that build up wildlife habitat. He contributes to and supports the planting of mast- and fruit-producing trees, winter cover crops and streambank protection. Through various clubs and agencies and contributions and activities, the hunter has purchased and leased countless thousands of acres specifically for the protection and enhancement of game and non-game wildlife species. Through his represen-

Proud father shows son how wing reveals whether boy's first mourning dove is juvenile or adult.

tatives he has prevented the passage of much legislation that would be detrimental to wildlife, while at the same time promoting the sound legislation that has formed the basis and progress of our beneficial conservation and environmental measures. The hunter has sponsored youth conservation clubs, hunter safety clubs and training schools. He has helped to sponsor and finance summer camps and has given of his experience and leisure time to teach youngsters how to get along with and appreciate their natural surroundings. In other words, the hunter plays an enormous part in wildlife conservation.

But, like a prickly thistle in a bunch of daisies, there's the occasional guy who, though he pays his taxes and buys his license and such, nevertheless hurts the sport by his shoddy behavior. Maybe you can recall some of these fellows: The guy who leaves his empty hulls and sandwich wrappers at his shooting stand; the one who leaves every gate open; the fence-rider-downer; the farm-buildings-and-livestock-pepperer; the beverage-can-in-the-pond-thrower; the one who drives his car across fields of standing grain, or cleans his doves and leaves the feathers and entrails to smell up the fencerow. I can think of others but they're pretty much alike. It would be quite proper to correct the next one you see.

But generally, hunters can be credited for the good they do. The rule is, simply, "If you play, you pay," because you're shooting game that belongs to all of the public. This is how it is in America; it is definitely not so in other countries. The hunter should expect to pay for his privilege by helping to restore and preserve that which he uses at public expense, and the public might try to appreciate the hunter's contribution. The hunter and non-hunter can and do exist harmoniously when each tries to understand and acknowledge the other's desires and contributions.

2
Life History of The Dove

Physical Characteristics

Size: It may surprise some — and especially the shooters — to learn that the length and width of a dove is about 12 inches, tail tip to beak tip or wing tip to wing tip. This is a lot of feather space. To a shooter, the bird is a flying object that occupies as much space as a sheet of paper, yet is harder to hit than a clay target less than half as big. Weight during September and October hunting seasons averages four ounces for juveniles and five ounces for adults — about an ounce lighter than a bobwhite quail. Doves may range from three to six ounces but these are extremes. You can't separate adults from juveniles or males from females by weight because there is so much overlap. Young squabs just out of the nest may weigh more than the parents.

Color: Call it gray and buffy-brown with

Doves may roost during midday heat but will fly again in afternoon to feed and then go to water.

34 · The Dove Shooter's Handbook

Typical mourning dove is a trim bird that measures about 12 inches from bill tip to end of long tail.

black spots and white feather tips. There are light and dark phases in the usual coloration of the mourning dove. You might find an extra-light or an extra-dark dove. Some researchers have attempted to separate different races by their light or dark appearance. In adults you can fairly dependably separate the sexes by color if you make an effort to learn the differences. The adult male's head has a blue tone on the top and back, whereas the female's head is mostly brownish. The neck feathers

Life History of The Dove · 35

of the male are purplish, gold, metallic, iridescent. The female's, again, are mostly brownish. This iridescent feather tract is nearly two inches long in the male and seldom longer than one inch in the female when present at all. The sex ratio is about 50–50, as many males as females.

Albino Doves: The genetic condition known as albinism—a deficiency or absence of pigmentation—is occasionally seen in individual birds and mammals of many species. At a distance, it's impossible to tell whether a very light-colored mourning dove is a true albino. Most that I've seen were an off-white color, somewhere between light tan and creamy, with the normally dark spots in the wings and body being comparatively lighter. A dove this color could be an albino or a dominant white.

A true albino lacks all pigment, so even the eyes, toes and bill appear pinkish. The dominant white is a white strain or race and will have the normal eye color. A black phase, called melanistic, is biologically possible. Melanism is common in some animals. I've never seen an all-black mourning dove, but I did see one with a very dark, sooty-colored neck, breast and feet.

Size and Color of Whitewings: Although whitewings occupy a limited range and account for a relatively small percentage of the nation's dove

Unusual dove at left, though not true albino, is dominant white strain; at right is normal color.

Life History of The Dove · 37

Wings at top display pale hue of most so-called albinos; normal wings are shown for comparison.

shooting, Southwestern hunters should be able to recognize them. Sportsmen in this region sometimes go out specifically for white-winged doves and sometimes simply include them in a shoot along with mourning doves.

The average whitewing is just a trifle larger than a mourning dove and is differently marked. It has a stockier body although, like the mourning dove, it's smaller and more streamlined than a common pigeon. It has dark brownish-gray primaries and secondaries and big, white, sharply contrasting patches on the wing coverts. Its tail is blunt rather than pointed, and the rear corners of

Even when perching, white-winged dove is easily identified by strip of white along edge of wing.

the tail are tipped with white. Even when the bird is roosting or feeding rather than flying, a strip of white is visible on each wing.

Feather Molt: Doves complete a feather molt once a year. It is believed that molting generally occurs in mourning doves from May through October, but I have found juveniles as well as adults molting primary flight feathers in December and January. Molting in doves doesn't seem to interfere with egg-laying, flying or any other activity, as it does in some other birds. This is probably

Life History of The Dove · 39

because the molt is progressive—involving a few feathers at a time.

Studies of wing molt have revealed definite patterns that have been used in aging doves—up to the time they molt their last primary feather. Doves have 10 primaries. Starting with the innermost at the first bend in the wing as number 1, count outward through 10. This is the way they are molted. Beginning at about 30 to 40 days of age, the primary flight feathers are replaced one at a time. In both wings, the corresponding feathers— say primary feather number 5 in the left and right wings—will be shed and replaced at the same time.

Each wing feather is replaced in about 10 days, so in roughly 150 days or five months a young mourning dove will have completed its post-juvenile molt. From then on, for all practical purposes, the feathers are the same as those of an adult. It is true that you may see two different primary feathers being molted at the same time—say, for instance, number 3 and number 8. The simultaneous molting of feathers that far apart would definitely be out of natural sequence so in all probability it would be due to an injury. An accident would not necessarily affect both wings, so number 3 might be molting on both sides and number 8 only on one side. Since the accidentally lost feather would be replaced at normal speed, it's logical to ask if the new feather, number 8, would be shed again when its turn came just a little while later. Seems unlikely, but I don't know for sure.

The investigation of feather molt has been enlightening. Many secrets were revealed by the studies. A molt-rate table, devised by several workers with wild and with known-age doves, is provided on pages 42–43 to help you age your doves. In most cases you can date your dove reasonably near to the date it was hatched by comparison with the table. This is only for birds of the year, but as I pointed out in the first chapter, average longevity is less than 12 months. (Mortality factors will be discussed later in this chapter.)

Aging Doves: Most of the doves you shoot will be young ones. To separate old from young mourning doves, look for white tips or fringe on the feathers. The younger the dove, the more white-tipped feathers. The primary coverts—the smaller feathers covering the flight feathers—are white-tipped and each one is molted just before the long primary feather under it. If the bird is molting primary number 5, chances are that the covert over number 6 is being replaced by one without a white tip. When the 10th primary feather and the covert are molted, there are no more white-tipped feathers and the dove is then considered an adult. But you can still spot a probable

Life History of The Dove · 41

Three wings at top are from mature doves; light feather tips show wings at bottom are juvenile.

bird of the year that has completed its molt if you examine the three outermost feathers. If they are new, not faded or frayed, chances are good that it is a young dove that has completed its molt. To be more exact requires internal inspection. So to age your dove you first determine whether it is a juvenile by the white feather tips, then determine which primary feather is being replaced, then go to the table and find the age in days and the probable hatching date.

Aging techniques help researchers learn

about population dynamics and other concerns of game management, but why should hunters ever bother to age birds? The answer is that hunters are admirably curious; they care about their game and want to learn all they can about it. Scratch an avid hunter and you're apt to find an amateur naturalist.

Table for Aging Juvenile Doves

This table is based on known-age (banded) wild doves recaptured and on studies of wing molt in wild and captured birds by John M. Allen in Indiana, James H. Jenkins in Georgia and Wendell G. Swank in Texas (see Selected Bibliography). To age your dove, determine which of the 10 primaries was the latest feather molted. It will be new-looking, more freshly colored than the others. Locate that number in the first column and read across. As noted above the third column, the estimated hatch dates are for birds shot on September 10 — a typical opening day. Suppose you bag a dove 10 days later — on September 20 — with the number 5 primary molted; it will still be 50 to 79 days old, as shown in the second column, but its probable hatch date was July 20, or 10 days later than the July 10 date shown in the third column. Thus a calendar and a bit of easy arithmetic will give you the hatch date for doves shot later in the season. But remember, this table is only for young doves. Those that have completed the molt of all 10 primaries cannot be accurately aged.

Life History of The Dove · 43

Primary Feather Number	Days Old—(from date of hatch)	Estimated Hatch Date (for birds bagged on Sept. 10)
0	22–39	August 11
1	24–54	August 8
2	25–49	August 2
3	36–59	July 24
4	38–66	July 17
5	50–79	July 10
6	64–86	June 26
7	64–94	June 22
8	86–125	May 29
9	125–134	May 1
10	125–150	April 23

Kentucky game biologists examine hunters' kills for age, general condition and possible disease.

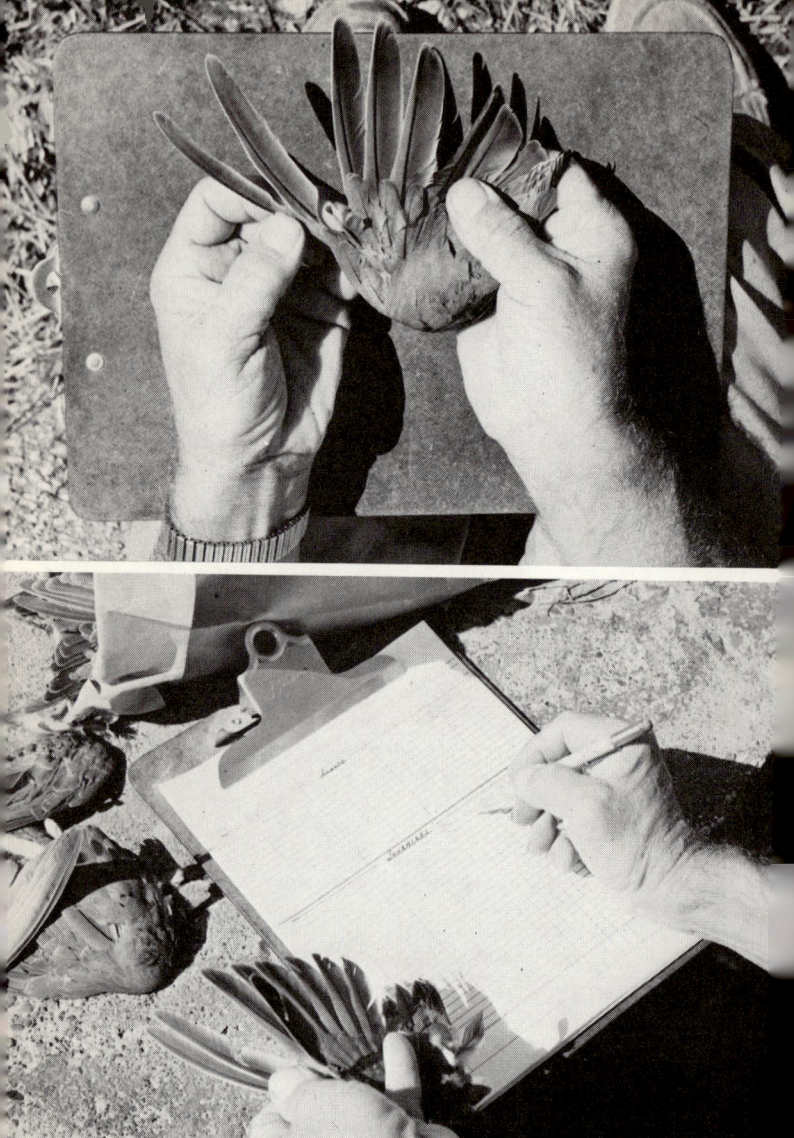

Ages are recorded in management study; wing at top, missing primary number 8, is nearly four months old.

Life History of The Dove · 45

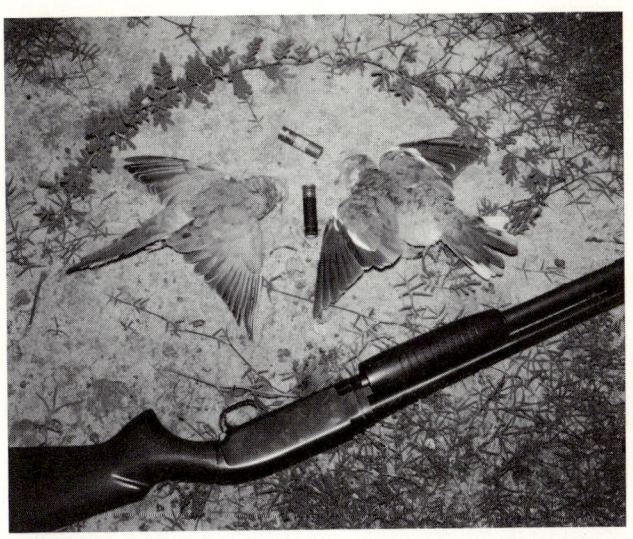

Mourning dove is at left, whitewing at right; note differences in tail contour as well as in markings.

Range and Habitat

Doves seem to have benefitted from modern farming methods and development of urban areas, while other birds such as quail and grouse moved out as human activity increased. Doves have adapted to such extent that studies in some areas have shown a larger portion of their population is produced in towns or other man-made or man-influenced environment. Doves are highly mobile, and they like openings, large fields and sparse trees in open land or edge for nesting.

Nesting Range: The nesting range of mourning doves includes every state in the continental U.S. (except Alaska) plus southern Canada as well as Central Mexico and Cuba. Their migratory habits are not so easy to define. It appears that some of the more hardy birds like to spend the winter at home, regardless of where it is or how cold it gets. Some like to move south a short way while others move very far into the Deep South for the winter. Generally speaking, most of them winter in the southern half of the U.S. Eastern doves concentrate chiefly in the southeastern Gulf states. Western flocks winter in the Southwest and Mexico. Frederick C. Lincoln, the government biologist mentioned before, wrote of an incident in 1921 involving some hunters in Georgia who disagreed with the federal regulations and attempted to prove the dove to be a resident species and therefore not subject to the federal migratory-bird regulations. But the federal Court at Athens, Georgia, decided it was migratory and as such entitled to the protection afforded by the Migratory Birds Treaty Act, "even though individual doves may remain yearlong within the borders of certain states." And that's the way it is.

Perhaps this individuality in doves is part of

the reason for their survival and well-being. No matter how cold it gets, food and shelter are the factors that determine survival in all wild things. If these needs are not met, the dove can move, fast and far. (But they do sometimes get caught with their feathers down, as we shall see later.

Whitewing Distribution: White-winged doves in the U.S. breed chiefly in lower California and Nevada, Arizona, New Mexico and Texas. There are two races, and the more easterly variety occasionally shows up as far east as Florida, but not in significant numbers. The whitewing, like the mourning dove, is migratory. Flocks begin to leave their nesting range in early autumn — hence the September season — and many of them, especially those in the lower part of the nesting range, are below the Mexican border as early as October.

Nesting

Wherever it decides to call home, a dove is likely to find suitable space and accommodations for nesting — open land or on the edge of a forest or woodlot, in town, in a backyard, in a cemetery, along a creek or on a window ledge or in the back seat or on the dash of an abandoned auto. Usually the mourning dove builds within 12 feet of the ground, but I've found nests more than 40 feet up in an oak or evergreen. I've also found nests in such out-of-the-way places as a ball of old wire fence, on an open shelf or rock in a quarry and under a ledge of rock in a strip-mine pit. I've found only a couple of nests on the ground but have read of them and received reports of ground-nesting. The stories you read of the famed passenger pigeons nesting in colonies so thickly packed together they weighed down the limbs of trees certainly don't apply to their mourning-dove cousins. Mourning doves are gregarious but apparently not in nesting. Anything approaching colonial nesting would be rather unusual.

Modern farming methods and agricultural practices, more grain, large fields—these all are generally beneficial to doves. There seems to be no shortage of nesting space except perhaps in the more arid regions of the Southwest. There, some of the streamside clearing practices are reducing available nest space, but I understand this is most damaging to the white-winged doves.

Nesting Differences Between Mourning Doves and Whitewings: The whitewing, in contrast to the mourning dove, is pretty much a colonial nester; that is, it nests in groups the way the passenger pigeon used to. It usually produces only a couple of broods per year, and its nesting season—June, July and August—is much shorter than the mourning dove's. As you will note in the following

Most but not all dove nests are in trees; this one is under a ledge, on side of abandoned strip mine.

pages, the mourning dove in some regions has a nesting period almost three times as long and it produces more broods.

Since the birds are of the same family, it is to be expected that there are certain similarities in courting, nest construction, incubation, brooding and so on. However, from here on my discussion of nesting will be concerned specifically with mourning doves, not only because my own field work has been with these birds but because they are our most important game; they're the species most hunters mean when they speak of doves.

Nesting Territory: Most birds display some effort to defend their nesting territory but this trait isn't strong in doves. Still, I've never found two dove nests close together. I did once find two active nests in the same tree, but the tree was a large white pine and the nests were easily 30 feet apart. Doves are often found nesting in a confined area such as a small backyard, yet I never saw one try to defend the whole place as his territory. I do recall two confused females that were working on the same nest. A male flew to the ground near the nest and cooed and both females went down to him. He flew off with one and the other went back to the nest. Shortly, both females were back at the nest. The male seemed satisfied to let them work it out between them, or at least he didn't display any eagerness to split them up.

The most aggressive dove I recall was one that behaved like a barnyard rooster, chasing away all of 15 or 20 other doves trying to get to a pile of corn I had put out for them. In what I'd have to call a rare display of aggressiveness, it even chased away a purple grackle. But this was for food, not for a nesting site, and this dove was a female. I don't know of any scientific proof that females are more aggressive than males, but it's something to think about.

Do doves of the year mate? This is possible.

Doves hatched very early in the nesting season could attain sexual maturity before the end of the same nesting season, and certain findings suggest that it happens. We have found young of the year with swollen "milk" glands on the crop. More study might be done on this.

We can assume that all doves at the beginning of the nesting season have reached sexual maturity. Most of them were hatched during the previous season, and a few may be even older. It is the ones nesting in the late summer and early fall we may wonder about. Are they always mature doves making a final nesting attempt—perhaps their fifth or sixth in a long season—or are some of them birds of the year trying for their first brood?

Up until recently, January was the month when I expected to hear doves begin cooing. Usually in late January there comes a breath of spring, a warm chinook wind or such that seems to activate the calling of doves. Last year, several began calling about December 20 and kept it up all through a two week warm spell. I also heard one calling on November 24 and again on December 3 this past winter.

Courtship and Mating: Courtship is no big spectacle among doves—no dancing or jumping around and fighting off suitors as with some birds.

It is mostly billing and cooing, picking and preening. On occasion the male takes to the air to sail around in a great circle, then returns to his perch and calls. Mating occurs frequently from early courtship throughout the nesting period. I think it's safe to say most investigators feel that a given pair of doves will remain mates, paired through the nesting season, at least, but if one bird were lost the other would probably take a new mate. But new mate or old mate, the female is wooed and won at each nesting attempt.

There is some evidence that the male goes back to the female's choice of nesting area; that is, the instinct to go back to the home area to nest is dominant in the female.

Nesting Period: Usually in the Southeast, at least as far north as the Ohio River, nesting begins in February. The early nesting efforts are highly unsuccessful due to the storms at that time of year. But they go on, gaining intensity and success, toward a peak that may occur from mid-May to mid-July and then decline rapidly by mid-September. The earliest nest I found in my studies in Kentucky was on February 1, the latest on October 10. The peak was from May 10 to June 10. The nesting period may be somewhat longer in the Deep South and shorter in the North but the peak seems to occur at about the same time.

Nest Building: Doves are lazy nest builders. The pair finds a suitable crotch or flat fork or a platform of sufficient size. The male gathers nest materials, giving them to the female who then works them into the nest. Working at their leisure, mostly in the morning hours, they take about a week to get the nest ready and the two white eggs laid. Often the eggs can be seen from below, showing through the nest. Doves sometimes use old or abandoned nests of other species, and it is a fortunate clutch whose mother has picked an old robin nest or a similarly strong one. Doves seem to recognize the weakness of their nest structure and they are sometimes willing to utilize more sturdy foundations when available — or maybe it is just pure laziness.

Nest Material: Nests are made of whatever is handy — usually twigs, grass, sticks or straw. Ordinarily the material is rather heavy, thick twigs and such. Sometimes a dove can be amusingly stubborn about its choice. I was sitting on a rural county-courthouse lawn waiting for a fellow one June day when a dove flopped down out of a maple tree nearby. It picked up a grass stem and flew back up into the tree. I watched. In a moment it was back on the ground. This time it grabbed a rooted stem. It was entertaining to watch that dove, so determined to have that grass stem, rooted

Female is on nest; incubation takes two weeks, and her two eggs will hatch on successive days.

or not. I couldn't help wonder, if the silly bird thought it was strong enough to pull roots, why it didn't just break off some twigs near the nest site and pile them on.

Egg Laying and Hatching: Egg laying usually takes two days. One solid-white egg is laid each day, and since the dove begins incubation immediately, they hatch the same way — on two successive days. One squab is invariably a day older than the other, and until they are about grown you can see a difference in their size. The eggs hatch after an incubation period of about 14 days. The young are altricial; that is, they have to be cared for intensively by the parents. Most game birds are precocial — ready to scoot about as soon as they hatch. Sibling doves are ordinarily of the same sex. They are fed on "pigeon milk" (or in this case "dove milk"), a concentrated food material, a white granular curd secreted from glands on each side of the crop of each parent.

Both male and female feed the young by opening their beaks wide and expressing this milky curd material out into the throat. The young reach their bills in greedily to take the nourishment. After a few days the "milk" is mixed with small seeds. After about 10 days the diet is entirely made up of small seeds. Well-fed, fat young doves spend 10 days to two weeks in the nest, feeding and growing.

Sometimes the best place to watch dove activity is around your backyard. Be alert for pairs nesting nearby. Two young, hatched in my apple tree, liked to loaf on a concrete slab near the back door. They would come right up to the door, get on the step and soak up the sun. At feeding time the old dove would come to the edge of the slab and call them away, using the first note of the coo call in rather rapid, chopped-off "co-co-co-co" sounds that were very low but plainly audible up close. When they were far enough away to be safe, the parent would let the young begin their gluttonous feeding. Sometimes it looked as if they would

*Top: Mourning dove's eggs are about to hatch.
Bottom: First egg, 14 days old, has hatched.*

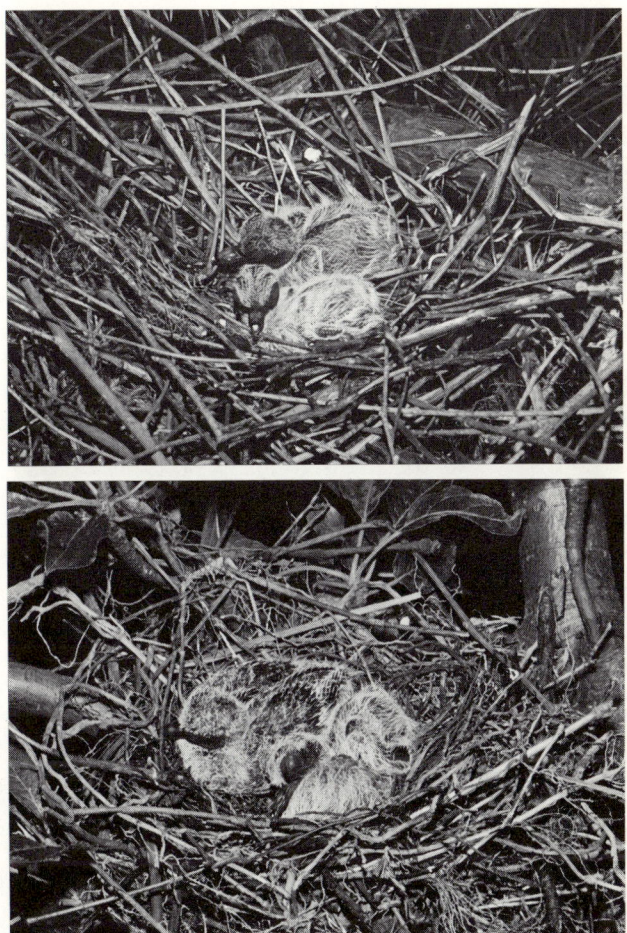

*Top: Chicks are shown at age of one and two days.
Bottom: Note development four days after hatching.*

Young mourning doves grow very quickly; bird is pictured at 11 days of age (top) and at 14 days.

To observe feeding behavior of young doves in his own back yard, author has put down corn for them.

surely tear the old dove's throat apart. The old dove remained wary throughout, and if I opened the screen or pulled aside the curtain the old dove would take off in a whirl and leave the young floundering around, wondering what kind of mixed-up parent they had.

Care of Young: Both parents take part in the incubation and feeding, and both are needed. If one parent is lost, it is doubtful whether the young will survive. The adults swap their vigil for food and water breaks but the male usually takes his stint on the nest from eight a.m. until four or five

Parent feeds nestling on "dove milk"—granular curd secreted from glands on each side of crop.

p.m., and the female then takes the night shift.

As with a number of altricial species, care of the young includes getting rid of egg shells that might attract predators to the nesting site. One day while I was driving along, a dove flew parallel to me. At first I thought it had a white head. Then it dropped what I saw was half of an egg shell and turned away from the road. Another time I was sitting on my back step watching a dove nest in a nearby pine tree. Suddenly the dove came diving out of the tree and buzzed over my head. It held a half-shell in its beak as it sped away from the nest.

In a few moments it was back in the pine, and there were no discarded shell fragments near the tree to give away the nest location.

Nest Success: Let's say a pair of doves builds a nest in February, but this first nest of the breeding season is destroyed by wind. Production so far is zero. The birds make another nesting attempt in March, and this time the female lays two eggs, both of which hatch. By and by the two young fly. We now have two nesting attempts, with 50 percent success but—because the second attempt brought two young rather than just one—the first failure is canceled out and the average production is one young per attempt. From February to September, the birds make repeated attempts to nest. Some attempts succeed, some fail, and the typical rate of success continues to average 50 percent while the typical rate of production averages one fledged young per nest attempt.

In most cases, there are two eggs per clutch. Occasionally only one egg is laid. In a nesting study that I carried on for something over three years, I recorded the success and production of about 600 nests. I found 11 nests with three eggs each. But whether a nest had one, two or three eggs, the overall production for the year was always the same, averaging one young produced per nest attempt. About half the nests were successful,

62 · The Dove Shooter's Handbook

Two eggs are normal, but author found two separate clutches of three eggs each in this Kentucky nest.

with one or more young produced to make up for the failures in the total average, thus maintaining a season-long rate of one dove hatched and reared per attempt. In other words, if I found 100 nests, I would expect some to fail but I would also expect to find that 100 young doves were raised.

In the 11 three-egg nests, 17 of the 33 eggs hatched and 11 young were produced. In one case the same nest was used twice in succession and each time there was a three-egg clutch. Five of the six eggs hatched but only two young reached fledgling size — again, one per nest attempt. The survival rate has been much the same in every study that I know of. I once found a nest with four

Oversized clutches like this — two hatched and two more eggs — do not raise average reproduction rate.

eggs, but I suspect that two females were using the same nest. Anyway, I later found two eggs on the ground, broken. The other two hatched and developed successfully.

One nest I located was used four times in a row. My notes read: "Nest number 27. Nest attempt February 28; abandoned after a storm on March 12." The nest was repaired and: "A second attempt made on April 1. April 28, adult feeding two young. Young flew April 30. May 3, adult back on nest. Young flew from tree May 29. July 11, adult again on same nest. July 27, nest empty and deserted." No doves were seen there after that date. Results: Four nest attempts, four young produced. In all, I kept records on over 600 nests. The success average was 49 percent, with an average production of one young per nest attempt.

Normally the adults can keep the droppings hauled away as long as possible — until the young get too big and too hungry. After that the rule is, feed the young and let the nest go. This is a good reason for building a new nest each time. Then, too, the large young practically tear the old nest apart before they are ready to fly off. They prepare themselves for flight by leaving the nest for periods of stretching, walking and wing-flapping. The period from egg laying to fledging is about a month — two weeks of incubation and two weeks of growing. A newly fledged dove stays around the nest area for some days after it can fend for itself, but the parents are through with it and they usually begin building another nest in a few days.

Nesting Mortality: As you would expect, the nesting period is the time of the greatest loss of mourning doves. Five percent of the nests are abandoned before any eggs are laid. Most nest losses (about 35 percent) occur while eggs are present. Then, one out of ten (ten percent) are broken up while young are present, bringing the total failures to about half of the attempts. As mentioned, storms and weather take a toll, but nests also are destroyed by bluejays, grackles, squirrels, flying squirrels, hawks, crows, ants, snakes and miscellaneous wildlife. In one case I feel certain that large black ants were the direct cause of death of two young. Often ants are seen in a nest after eggs are broken or the young have died, but on this morning I saw the ants and live young in the nest. That evening I checked it again and both young were dead. Circumstantial evidence, admittedly, but I was convinced.

Artificial Nests: Prefabricated nests for doves? The idea of providing artificial platforms has been tried, and it works. Tar-paper cones and wire-mesh cones have been used by doves. As an experiment I also wired small woven-bamboo baskets up in trees and some were used successfully.

Multiple Broods: Doves are our only game birds that set out to raise several broods in one season. A pair may make four to six nest attempts, about half of them successful. As I've pointed out in the discussion of nest success, the failures are offset in the overall average by the frequent raising of two young rather than one, so that 50 percent success results in an average of one young per nest. Therefore, since a pair may make four to six attempts, two mated doves may produce four to six young in a single breeding season.

Reproductive Potential: While the observed nesting success is only about 50 percent, doves have a potential to recover severe losses. Back in the winter of 1950–51, when the big freeze was so severe throughout the Southeast that even the mobile doves couldn't escape it, starvation and disease took a heavy toll of the wintering population, and the following spring census counts dropped to half of the estimated normal level. But by the end of the second year after that lethal winter the population level appeared to be almost fully recovered.

Foods and Feeding Habits

Here again, I'm going to center my discussion on the mourning dove, the most important member of the dove family. But first I'd better say a few words about whitewings for those who are unfamiliar with them. As I mentioned in the introduction to this book, whitewings aren't much different from mourning doves in their requirements and behavior. Whitewings have adapted well to rather arid land, and in unsettled areas or ranch country they rely on weed fields and a variety of wild foods to a greater extent than the farm-country mourning doves. But, like mourning doves, whitewings have also learned to use cultivated cereal-type grains, sometimes to the dismay of local farmers during periods of peak whitewing population.

Proso millet field will be shot over, then left as is to feed doves, other game and non-game species.

Terms of 10 and even 20 miles have been given in estimating the distance whitewings may fly to water. Their preferred or required habitat is not as extensive as that of mourning doves, and their requirements for nesting space and water in some regions are in considerable conflict with agricultural needs. Streamside clearing and the clearing and burning of large mesquite thickets in their arid habitat is believed to be a serious menace to their well-being. Still, the similarities between the species outweigh the differences. An experienced dove shooter knows that birds of either kind are most likely to be found where they can feed on grain or wild seeds, where they can pick grit, where they can get water or where they can roost. Having made that clear, I'll concentrate now on mourning doves.

Ordinarily you shouldn't say of any wild creature that it won't do this or won't do that. Because the next time you see one it may be doing just what you said it "won't" do. All the same, I've never seen or read of a dove scratching for food or even picking grain off a seed head or an ear of corn. All the food I've seen them take was lying free on the ground or, in the case of bait for trapping, on a cement slab or board, always in the open and available to be picked up without scratching. Usually, the cleaner the feeding surface is, the better they like it.

I watched a hungry dove stand by while a purple grackle pulled kernels off an ear of corn but the dove never attempted to do the same for itself. But then I was surprised one day to find a dove perched on a bird feeder that was hanging from a limb about five feet off the ground, taking small seeds out of the slot.

Preferred Foods: The mourning dove's diet consists mostly of cultivated crops—corn and small grains, milo, wheat, sorghum, millet, peas, peanuts and the like. Weed and grass seeds are used heavily, especially the smaller varieties. During the hunting season the birds' crops are often found full of dove weed (*Croton* spp.), pig-weed (amaranthus spp.), bull grass (paspalum) and wild millet, or barnyard foxtail (*Chaetochloa* spp.) They seem to prefer the smaller seeds of the wild plants. Of the cultivated foods wheat, milo, sorghums, and corn are used most heavily.

It is becoming a common practice to do some planting to attract doves for shooting. Up until very recently it has been strictly taboo—against

Combined milo field is valuable type of shooting site; farm crops are vitally important to doves.

regulations to bait doves in any fashion. (And since regulations are subject to change from year to year, I wouldn't recommend that you do any crop planting or manipulating without first checking to make sure that what you propose to do is legal.) But lately, with the justified relaxation of restrictions, more special planting is being done, and with excellent results.

For a long time now it has been okay to plant things like millet, milo-maize and such, specifically to attract doves to shoot—so long as you did nothing to it but let it stand. To have the seed readily available to the doves, the planter usually skipped two or three rows, leaving a wide bare strip between rows which he kept clean by cultivating. When the seed ripened, it fell on the clean, bare ground; and the doves did (and do) appreciate that kind of consideration. More recently the regulations have been relaxed to allow some manipulation of these standing dove-food plantings. But as I cautioned, it must be checked every year to see whether what you might wish to do is legal.

I've been asked about sunflower seed, and whether it really is a super food for doves. I have seen the fields and heard much about their success, which is great. However, a biologist in a state where sunflower is planted each year has advised me that in his opinion the sunflower is no greater

Camouflage-suited hunter pauses near edge of millet field to study mourning-dove foods.

attractant than millet, milo, etc., if these foods are equally distributed or made similarly available to the birds. I think that some wild plants or weeds might be better attractants if one wished to cultivate them for doves. For example, the crotons are called "dove weed" because the birds are so fond of them. And the tiny black seeds of pig-weed (amaranthus spp.) must be delightful to doves the way they pack hundreds of them in their crops at one feeding. The old-timers tell me that back during World War II when farmers were growing hemp for rope fiber, the doves went wild over that seed. This could be, it really could. But the leaves of hemp are now called pot, and raising that for dove food could get a fellow in big trouble.

I once watched some doves working in a burned-over field. Through my binoculars I noticed that some were picking up small snail shells. The probable reason would be the calcium content; for grit the birds would select harder material—gravel and sand. A craving for minerals isn't surprising; many animals visit mineral licks. I have often observed squirrels, rabbits and deer lapping up dust from a crushed-limestone road, and the only purpose I could imagine was for the minerals. For the same reason rodents gnaw on old bones and antlers, and many species of birds are known to ingest mollusk shells.

Shooter in lush Tennessee field pulls down fast-flying dove that came streaking in low.

One winter I began feeding a couple of doves in my backyard. More kept coming in until the flock numbered about 20. I put shelled corn out at night after they went to roost and they'd be there feeding in the morning. I don't recall how many bushels I shelled out for them but they used up to three ears a day for about two months. They would fill up quickly, swallowing the large kernels. They picked it up and slammed it down with a few jerks of the head. Then they'd go perch on my woodpile to loaf and soak up the winter sunshine — and mess up my pile of firewood. I've also watched doves in swampy woods and farm woodlots picking up small acorns and pieces of squirrel cuttings. And they learned quickly to visit the base of a tree where I stuck an ear of corn for the squirrels. A squirrel will cut the germ out of a kernel, then drop the rest of the grain in pieces. I've often seen one or more doves waiting for the squirrel, so they could get the cuttings.

Doves winter around feedlots, barns, cultivated fields and in woods next to these places. There they can usually find enough waste feed and grain and seed to sustain them.

As I've seen it, food and water have posed no great problem in mourning dove management. There are occasionally drastic winters and natural occurrences that smack the dove population a rough blow but such calamities can hardly be anticipated or prevented by a management program. I say "as I've seen it," because I recall mentioning this once several years ago in a conference paper and a short time later I received a letter from a college student who had some objections to my statement. Still, it is the combination of mobility and wide choice of food that tends to guarantee the dove a good living.

Grit: Doves pick up grit to grind against seed in the gizzard, a digestive organ surrounded by very powerful muscles. Sand and small gravel is picked up on a roadside or along a stream or in a field where they feed. With enough seed and grit to fill their crops they usually fly to water, then back to the roost or resting perch, or to a sunny patch of grass if the weather is cold or windy.

Water: Have you ever watched a dove drinking? The species is not like a chicken or quail or most birds that dip and then throw their heads back to let the water run down the throat. A dove dips its beak in and keeps it there while sucking up the water. When it lifts its head it is through drinking. Water is more critical then usual during periods of drought or freeze-up; then the birds must go to rivers or streams or domestic and industrial outlets. Even so, they seem to prefer dirty, brackish or stagnant water. As in feeding, they like

76 · The Dove Shooter's Handbook

Whitewing visits gravel patch; like other birds, doves use grit to grind seed in their gizzards.

to have a clear place to land on and go to water. The water may look filthy but they insist on a bare surface next to it. Check this factor if your pond isn't attracting doves.

Salt: Doves evidently like salt. They may get calcium from snail shells and they may get other minerals in their seed and grit, but such sources don't seem to provide all the salt they want. They often hang out around a livestock salt lick. A few years back it was illegal to shoot doves at a salt block or lick. They are commonly seen around the salt-water ponds at oil wells, and I have often seen shooters at these places. I recall a controversy in the news once about whether salt should be put out for birds because it might be harmful to them, but doves do seem to crave it at times.

Pesticides: Modern farming practices seem greatly beneficial to doves except for the increased use of insecticides and herbicides. Some sprays of the "pre-emergent" type that prevent weeds from growing between crop rows deprive birds of the natural foods such as wild millet (foxtail), ragweed and such. Doves don't eat much animal matter so they are relatively free from the secondary insecticide poisoning caused by eating killed bugs and worms. At least they are less victimized than worm-eaters like robins and woodcock, or the hawk and other birds of prey that come in at the dirty end of the food chain by eating animal tissues in which poisons have accumulated.

Population and Mortality Factors

Migration: In doves, the migratory process is not a sharp general breaking up of housekeeping and booting out the young and heading south for the winter. It is more gradual and less orderly. Some workers believe that the more advanced young doves tend to move out ahead of the adults.

We don't know whether they have a definite destination or whether they just stop in any good habitat. Migration seems to be scattered and gradual and somewhat divided by age groups. Juvenile doves begin flocking together and randomly moving about as early as the small-grain harvest is begun, usually early June. In August and September the movement is more general, with the older doves completing their nesting and joining the flocks. In most states where I've made observations or contacted other observers, the doves migrate in late September and early October. There is really no need for them to go before this. The harvest is in full swing, plenty of food is available, the weather is warm. But at the first cold snap, say a miserably cold rainy couple of days in September, doves leave—as most hunters can attest. I've also noticed doves move out of an area for no apparent reason; it must simply have been time to go. Then, too, I've missed seeing doves in an area they'd been using and found they'd moved into heavy cover nearby.

When they do migrate they don't all go all the way to the Deep South. The shift has been described as a "leap-frog" movement wherein the Northern doves moved into the middle of the country, the mid-country doves to the mid-South and mid-South doves to the Deep South. This was indicated in a study of band returns. But some of the doves from the uppermost areas do go to the far southern reaches of the range, sometimes in a long, fast, direct flight, wasting no appreciable time along the way.

Eventually the patterns will be worked out in detail from the many thousands of records of doves banded and recovered in the past 20 years or so. We hope we may even be able to distinguish the local segments of a state's population. Once it is possible to connect a given group of doves with their summer and winter range, the management possibilities are much more nearly complete. You can see how much more effectively we might protect a local flock or group if their exact summer and winter range could be pinpointed. It would then be a simple matter to restrict shooting where a particular segment of the population was known to be at a low level. There are active studies of the movement patterns at the present time.

For management purposes the U.S. is now divided into three sections called Management Units. These are described in the Management Section of this book. Doves usually move north and south within the broad confines of these units, and they don't cross into another unit often enough for concern. The ultimate aim is to determine where any group of doves will go within a unit.

Spring and Summer Movements: Doves come back to local areas in the spring to nest. The survivors of the winter pair off as early as late January. Nesting is a full-time business, and when it reaches a peak about mid-May to mid-June the population is most stable and considered to be in its home range. As the young leave the nests they begin gathering into flocks which are largest in late August or September.

Production Peak: The population is never stable. Peak numbers are no sooner reached than they are on the decline. With production stepped up, the momentum produces for a time more young than are lost, and the numbers soar. Then, as production slows, the factors of decline begin to take over: Hunting, predators, accidents, sickness, weakness, poisons, weather—all the limiting forces act together on the large population. Shooting, of course, takes a heavy toll and there's no way of knowing whether a bagged dove might have survived to the next nesting season. But sophisticated kill surveys and population estimates from banding records show that far more doves are lost each year than can be accounted for by hunter kill.

Annual Population Turnover: The annual replacement, or turnover, ranges from 60 percent to 80 percent in a given location in a given year. Of those that survive the first year, over half will not

Life History of The Dove · 81

Biologist, checking to see if doves are still breeding, confirms presence of "milk" glands.

live through a second year; and again, over half the remainder will not be around after the third year. An individual dove may be lucky enough to live much longer, but the life expectancy for seven out of ten doves is less than one year.

Predators, weather, disease, together or individually, seem to take the largest toll. Hunting takes its share. Sometimes all the factors seem to combine to reduce the flocks. For example, bad weather and ice storms may freeze up food supplies, and the doves become weak from hunger and thirst; then diseases, ever present, break out of the dormant stage due to the weakened condition of the cold and hungry birds. And, with doves concentrated on the wintering grounds, disease spreads more rapidly.

Diseases

Trichomoniasis: The microscopic organism *Trichomonas gallinae,* a one-celled flagellate shaped like a comma, with a round head and whiplike tail, is commonly found in doves and pigeons. It has also been found in barnyard fowl—turkeys and chickens—as well as in hawks. Sometimes called "roup" or "canker," it has evidently been recognized for a long time. Some strains of the organism are more virulent than others. Some might kill a dove within a few days, others in hours, and some strains might never kill the host dove. A really bad general infection of flocks (called an epizootic) can thin out a population. It may be transmitted in feeding and watering areas. Ever watch a dove or a chicken feeding? It will often pick up a grain and drop it and then pick up the same grain or another. Each time a grain is picked up it might become contaminated with the infective organism. A healthy bird, picking up the grain contaminated by the saliva of a sick bird, becomes infected. The disease can also be transmitted directly to nest-

Life History of The Dove · 83

This nest is in peach orchard, where study showed that insecticides hadn't lowered nesting success.

lings by the parent dove when the young feeding on pigeon milk take their food from the adult's mouth.

In this disease, small, yellow, cheezy-looking lumps occur in the mouth and throat. These "cankers" grow fast and may plug up the food passages. More than once I've watched an infected dove trying to swallow a grain of corn. It would hold a grain in its beak and try to pick up another, but then the first grain would fall out.

If the disease doesn't kill the bird directly,

starvation is commonly noted. The bird becomes skinny. The breast bone or keel, sticks up like a sharp ridge, whereas a healthy bird has a plump breast. Other factors, such as freezing temperatures and wind, further weaken the bird and ultimately contribute to its death. A typical report: "Hardin County, May 12, 1961. Found two dead doves, nestlings, in one nest, 8 and 9 days old. Canker and emaciation evident cause of death." Another: "Dead doves (3) Trigg County, January 21, 1951. Found on barn floor under feed trough. Grain available but doves apparently starved to death. Topical examination revealed cheezy mass blocking throat."

Fortunately, the disease does not affect humans. If you should happen to cook a dove that has an unnoticed infection, the cooking heat kills the organisms. And if the dove has anything more than a mild infection you'll know it—it stinks!

Disease Treatment: Enough is known about the causative organism to possibly clear up trichomoniasis in a backyard flock by doping the water and feed. But this wouldn't be practical on winter-range areas, would it? So doves, like all the rest of nature's creatures, have all sorts of enemies. It is nature's way of controlling excess populations of any species. When doves become crowded the disease thins them out just as rabies, distemper, tularemia and other diseases thin the numbers of various mammals. We don't know just how many doves the countryside can support but when they become too numerous for the available food and space, then—*wham!*—the disease, always present in some fashion, revives in the weaker birds and becomes active. Birds die off, sometimes their numbers go way down, until the population has room to move about without too much contact. The toughest birds survive to start another population cycle. So do the disease organisms. The procedure is repeated at intervals. There was a large outbreak of *T. gallinae* in 1950–51 and another in 1961. We don't know exactly what triggers it or just how often; it's possible that the disease takes a toll annually. The organism has been found in pigeons and it is suspected they may act as reservoir hosts for the disease. Doves and trichomoniasis have been together for a long time; they will probably coexist and survive in cycles for a long time to come.

Fowl Pox: Another disease of doves is a virus pox, which causes little wart-like nodes on the toes, beak or about the head. Less is known about the effects of this disease, called fowl pox, than about the *T. gallinae*. There is some indication that it may kill nestlings. I've seen many doves with the nodules that didn't seem to be hampered by it.

I've handled them, too. Admittedly I have on occasion had a wart or two. But I doubt there was any connection. My warts probably came from the toad-frogs I'd handled!

Predators

As you would imagine, the greatest loss to predators is during the nesting season, when there are untended eggs, helpless nestlings, adults on scheduled movements. Fledged doves, after they get out of the nest, are much safer. At trapping stations we have had to watch out for an occasional Cooper's hawk or sharp-shinned hawk, and sometimes a mink or weasel would raid the traps. Mostly, though, the raiders were dogs and cats. During hunting season, man takes a heavier toll than any other predator but this is believed not to be a limiting factor; it does not endanger the over-all population. There is an unexplained loss of greater proportions, apparently due to a combination of natural causes.

Parasites

The dove has its share of internal and external parasites, surely, but they don't appear to be of importance as to population levels. I was watching a young dove preening itself and suddenly it started digging its bill into its feathers like a dog after

Life History of The Dove · 87

a flea. Probably it had lice. Pests such as lice, fleas, etc., could be alternate hosts for certain diseases, and with other factors such as hunger and disease, they could be contributing causes of mortality.

Pesticides

One of my colleagues conducted a special study to determine nesting success and survival of young in a large peach orchard. For peaches as for other fruit, producers use several sprays, intensively working every tree over and over the year around. It was surprising to find that nesting suc-

This toeless dove was found in researcher's trap; it was victim of dry gangrene caused by freezing.

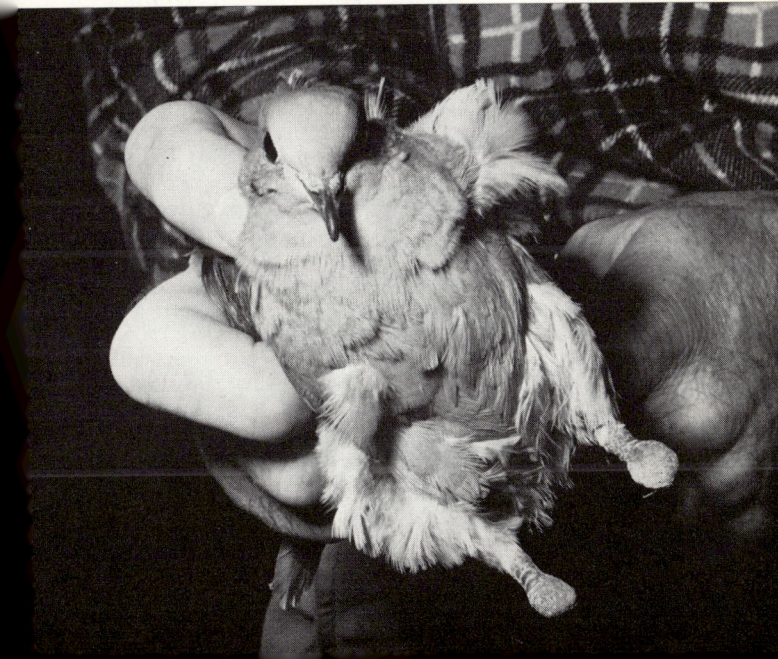

cess was just about the same in the orchard as elsewhere. One nest in a low fork was found with two dead nestlings, and death was attributed to a dousing with a highly toxic basal trunk spray. As mentioned previously, doves probably don't make enough use of insects to get a lethal dose of insecticide in their diet, but the seed merchants' practice of treating seed with dieldrin and other hard pesticides could be very dangerous. If the poison-coated seed is sown from a plane, a common practice today, or left on top of the ground accidentally where the birds can get at it, not many grains are needed to kill a dove or any other bird. Laboratory studies have proved this. The poison coating is intended to protect the seed while in storage but the poison is still highly effective when sown. The chemicals also may remain in the soil for an unlimited time afterward, posing additional dangers. For this reason most of the hard pesticides are banned from government lands managed primarily for wildlife. But birds can hardly be expected to know the difference between private and government-owned lands.

Weather

Have you ever seen a bob-tailed dove? This is rather common in some areas. Freezing rain, falling while doves are on the roost, literally ice-welds the tail feathers to a limb or the ground. In freeing themselves, they pull the tail feathers out. The feathers grow back in about a month or six weeks. I've also noticed breast feathers pulled out, and of course any feathers that touched a hard surface could be frozen to it. The feet can also freeze. A researcher found a toeless dove in a trap one morning; it had just a round ball on the end of each leg. It could stand and fly and was in fairly good shape otherwise, but it couldn't perch on a limb. The toes had dropped off from what was called dry gangrene. Freezing had cut off the circulation to the toes and they had simply sloughed off. Many times since, we have found doves with one or more toes missing but this was the most extreme case. Mobile doves can normally find shelter and sustenance at feed lots or barns or frozen cornfields in the North as well as in the more open feeding areas in the South. But when an ice storm hits or a hard winter slips way down into the Deep South, freezing up where it is not supposed to, shutting off the easy food supplies—and when a disease breaks out among the big flocks of starving birds concentrated on the wintering grounds—a great number of them will be wiped out. And this is what management people watch for. Fortunately, some of the hard-headed, cold-tolerant, disease-resistant, home-staying doves will survive, will

Shooter empties crop of bird he has downed in order to find out what grains doves are concentrating on.

turn on their full reproductive potential and recoup the losses in rapid order, as they did in the Southeast after the winter of 1951.

Behavior

Doves spend most of their time loafing, either in trees or on the ground. They pick and preen, sleep and eat. In summer they seldom congregate except at water holes or at a handy feeding area. The young form small flocks in June when small-grain harvests begin. As summer fades, the flocks grow larger. The adults, just finished nesting, still stay around separately or in loose groups. Once the cold weather comes, they seem to disappear. Actually they go South or into heavy cover. Large river bottoms are favorite wintering places. There they can find food in the crop residue. Woody swamps seem to be warmer and more protective and are favorite winter areas. I've often flushed large flocks of doves in deep woods in the winter. Doves water at ponds, oil-well catch basins, at creeks and rivers. They seem to enjoy their way of living and are either slow at catching on to new ways or prefer not to.

As well as they like to flock together, they can be individuals, too. One winter afternoon I watched a dove take his fill of corn, then waddle back to a patch of grass where the sun was shining and the wind was not hitting. He squatted in the dry grass, lifting one wing up and holding it so the sun shone on his breast and the underside of the wing. After a bit the dove got up, turned around and lifted the other wing for a sunning. Since that afternoon I've often noticed the same thing. It appears to be a common act.

One very hot July day I saw a dove alight in the middle of a bird-bath. It was something of a surprise to me as that was the first time I had seen a dove actually alight in the water. The bird waded all the way across and stepped up to the rim, then turned and waded back to the middle. It stretched and looked around, as if showing great concern for its privacy. Finally, convinced it was not being spied on (I almost expected to see it pull up its feathers), it dipped its breast down into the water, a little at a time, performed a little shuffle, then looked around again, giving the impression that it was conscious of this undignified act. It got its wings into the water several times but never, never let itself go to enjoy the bath like the "common" birds.

Something that takes getting used to is the difference in dove behavior during the summer — when the birds seem soft, cooing, tame creatures — and what you find in the fall and winter. Doves then are wind-burning, sky-splitting gray bullets. Summer bird-watchers and fall hunters would never agree on a description of these birds. Summer or winter, though, one thing is constant: When doves move, they move fast! I suspect this is just a symptom of their lazy nature. They probably don't like work, so they spend as little time as possible at it. They hurry to feed, they hurry to water, they hurry to roost. I've never seen one poking along in flight. Ever notice their steady wingbeat? They don't coast or sail or dip or fool around. They don't go unless there is a purpose. They would rather sit than fly, and, when they must fly, they do it in a big hurry so they can get back to sitting.

3
Dove Shooting

A Look Back at the Old Days

I witnessed only the last remnants of old-time dove shooting but, like most hunters in my part of the country, I've heard a lot about it. Big shoots were a tradition in the South, and they were lengthy "shootin', pickin' and partyin'" affairs, with no laws governing the season or the bag. For that matter, no laws governed the method, either, though custom as well as necessity dictated the use of shotguns. The take was limited only by the number of shells a man had on hand or how long he could keep at it before his shooting arm got too sore. Mostly it depended on the latter—how much bruising he could take—because only the fairly well-to-do could afford this kind of shooting for sport. The average farmer or other working man couldn't compete with the country gentleman, the banker or the wealthy merchant when it came to

Hunter rises out of weeds to take fast shot; flock will be out of range in another moment.

indulging in extended and extravagant social affairs that usually involved plenty of food, drink and ammunition.

The first real shooting controls resulted from the 1918 Migratory Bird Treaty, an agreement with Great Britain to protect and regulate the taking of birds moving back and forth between the United States and Canada. A law had been passed five years earlier giving the federal government the right to set closed seasons for migrating waterfowl, and some individual states had passed sensible game laws, but tighter regulation was needed. Since about the turn of the century there had been increasing pressure from conservationists — and particularly from sportsmen — to control the harvesting of game. Market hunting had taken a great toll, especially of waterfowl but of other game as well.

I suspect, too, that the movement for treaty legislation may have been given momentum by the demise of the passenger pigeon; the last one reportedly died in captivity in the Cincinnati Zoo in 1914. (Incidentally, this last bird was mounted and is now in the Museum of Natural History in Cincinnati. Some who have seen it — including myself — feel that this "last-of-a-species" should be better described and more prominently displayed.)

During the first year of protection under the

1918 treaty, bag limits were set at 25 doves per day. From that time on, restrictions have gradually taken the bag limit down. It reached a low of eight doves in 1951 and went back up to 18 doves in 1969 and 1970. It seems to have steadied now at 12 doves per day in the East, 10 in the Midwest and West; and I'd look for the limit to stay between 10 and 15 for some time to come. That's high enough, by comparison with the limits on most upland birds, to show that the dove populations are in good shape.

At this writing, the daily bag limit on mourning doves is 12 in the Eastern Management Unit, 10 in the Central and Western Management Units; the bag limit on whitewings is 10. In the Midwest and West, shooting is legal from half an hour before sunrise until sunset, while in the East it's from noon to sunset. Mourning-dove seasons generally last close to 70 days, some time between early September and mid-January, and some states split their seasons with a rest period between the early and late segments.

The limited range of whitewings in the lower Southwest is really just the top part of their breeding range, and they have only a relatively short distance to migrate before crossing into Mexico. By the end of a brief open season they're gone from the upper segment of the range. Moreover, they're less abundant than mourning doves, and the open season must be adjusted to the fluctuations in their numbers. Taking a typical year as an example, in 1972, Arizona's season was September 1 to September 12; California's three southernmost counties had a split season, all of September plus November 25 to December 10, and the remainder of the state was closed; in Nevada only two counties had an open season, but it ran from September 1 to October 20; New Mexico had a long split season—all of September plus November 18 to December 17; and in Texas, as usual, only certain areas opened a season and it lasted for just three days in early September, with legal shooting from noon to sunset instead of all day as in other parts of the West.

Modern Shooting

On several occasions I've watched and participated in some big dove shoots with, say, 300 people in the field and mourning doves coming in droves, shells popping like a string of firecrackers all up and down the line, birds falling, retrievers working, hunters yelling to each other, picking up birds, ducking low shots. It's quite a spectacle. In dove shooting now, except in a few instances where it is strictly for business promotion or for the head fees, the old country-style "Y'all come"

Hunters leave parking area and take to fields during typically big Southeastern dove shoot.

party-sport is fast disappearing. The shooting is still frantic but somewhat more under control.

On opening day, hunters string out across a field early. Some just have to be there the first minute, some older shooters are not so eager. They take their stand. By and by some of the young doves begin to get hungry and drop in to feed. Shooting starts sporadically at first, then it gets so steady you can't draw a full breath between shots. Wings whistle and the hunters' calls of "low bird" and "let 'em come in" mingle with hoots and jeers and "I gotta go get some more shells" and "mark 'em down, Junior" and "Fetch," and "How did I miss that one?" The shooting picks up as more doves come in to feed and more hunters, having heard the booming from a distance, arrive to join the shoot.

Everyone wonders sooner or later just how it is that a "dead" dove can keep right on flying. You have a clean shot and your aim is dead on, but the dove just flies on past. I recall one shoot in a combine-harvested cane-sorghum field. About 30 hunters were present and the shooting was sporadic. During a lull, a dove slipped in at one end of the field before it was seen. It zipped through the middle to the far end with every hunter unloading at it. Then, as if to prove a point, it banked and bore right back through the same air and again outmaneuvered the shots as it powered into the sun and disappeared over the line of trees. No wonder doves make such a contribution—in the form of the tax on ammunition—to the Wildlife Restoration Fund.

In the more northerly states, most of the dove shooting is over quite suddenly. The first open weekend in September catches the bulk of the season's hunting pressure. After a cold snap and some heavy shooting the doves get so wild and wary that fast bag limits aren't too common, and a lot of the hunters then quit. But there is still much good dove shooting to be had—with a little more patience and, of course, a little less crowd.

Just about anywhere, the first week or two of the season is apt to provide good shooting, but in those Southern states that open their seasons early the shooting remains good long after that. By October, however, most of the field harvesting is done and there is plenty of food for doves everywhere, in every field, in any direction. The birds don't have to concentrate to feed then and a single shot might spook a flock of doves clear out of the county. At this time pass-shooting is about all you can expect; still, pass-shooting in a high wind is quite a challenge.

Shooting over Feed: Favored shooting areas in early September are in harvested grain fields and around farm ponds. Once a flock of mourning doves has decided on a feeding ground—such as a wheat-stubble or sorghum field or corn cut for silage or a millet-bean hay field that has been cut and raked—they return regularly day after day. Doves gather on telephone lines and power lines and in trees near such fields. Hunters watch for these gathering places in order to locate the feeding grounds, and they usually have several such areas located by the opening date.

Hunters, ranging in number from one to a dozen or occasionally to a hundred or more, take their shooting stands at fence-corner posts, under

Shooter follows old tradition of Southern comfort; folding stool has compartment for birds or shells.

trees, in brushy fence rows or even in the middle of a field, using whatever cover is there. Some bring a portable blind. It takes several shooters in a large field to keep doves flying; otherwise the birds settle at the far end, feed, then pick up and leave. It doesn't take them long to finish feeding, once they get to it.

In September the weather is likely to be as hot as it was in August. Doves will "lay up" in the woods and thickets during the hot part of the day — until three or four o'clock in the afternoon. Then they fly out to feed, and after that to water and on to the roost. Young doves, like all young animals, move around more than the older ones. They fly about more and eat more often. An early-afternoon shoot at feeding areas usually means lots of young doves bagged. A late-in-the-day shoot around feeding areas and watering holes will usually show a larger percentage of older doves bagged. As an example, I checked two shoots one year on the second and fourth of September. At the first shoot, about five p.m., a total of 27 doves were bagged. Of the 27 birds, 19 were adults and 15 of these adults were in breeding condition, as determined by the glandular crop. At the second shoot, a much bigger affair that began at noon, 303 doves were examined. All but 23 were young birds; none were breeders.

As I mentioned earlier, whitewings aren't basically very different from mourning doves in their habits—or at least in those habits that influence a hunter looking for a good shooting station. As with mourning doves, the shooting is often very good in grain fields. However, as I also mentioned, whitewings in some regions depend more heavily on weed seeds and other wild foods. And they're so well adapted to arid country that the shooting can be excellent right out on the desert. One of their popular names, in fact, is "cactus dove." On the Arizona deserts where the strange-looking organ-pipe cactus grows, they often feed on the red

Waterhole shooting sometimes comes in sudden spurts; here, two shotgunners both pull down incoming birds.

cactus fruits that ripen at the time of the hunting season. Sometimes a shooter can stand in the shadow of a tall cactus and have fine sport as the doves come in.

Whitewings have a more deliberate style of flight than mourning doves and they don't appear to be traveling quite as fast, but that's probably an illusion. They can be tough targets, especially when they spot movement and flare. And they tend to fly high. At times maybe they're just passing through during migration and have no intention of coming down, but mostly it's just that they have to fly such long distances between roosts and feeding areas or watering spots. Some shooters like to station themselves on a hill or other elevation to get at least a little closer to the birds coming over. The sport is primarily pass-shooting, the same as with mourning doves.

Roost Shooting: When doves start to the roost, daylight is fading fast and "sunset time" by the clock on a cloudy day makes quitting time pretty near "smack-up dark," as they say. It's dark enough, anyway, to see the fire out of the end of the barrel and dark enough so you duck down to see the dove above the skyline, where it shows clearly enough to shoot. This poor visibility and the fast, frantic shooting makes the crippling rate high. And many of the birds that fall are lost. The

First doves arrive at roost in late afternoon, but good sportsmen quit shooting before sunlight fades.

doves become confused when cut off from the expected roost site, and it is usually too dark for them to go elsewhere. Then, too, on the ground or in an unfamiliar roost they are more subject to predator loss than they would normally be.

All this makes for too much waste. It's poor sport. Neither is it good management, as I see it, to allow this type of dove shooting. In all fairness to the hunters, I must add that I've seen many of them pass up roost shooting. Most of those I've questioned would just as soon have shooting stop a half-hour before sunset rather than wait out those last few minutes before legal quitting time.

Dove Shooting · 107

Stationed in ditch where birds can't see him until close, shooter swings on dove coming to farm pond.

Water-Hole Shooting: Doves also flock up at watering places, ponds, creeks, salt-water wells and river banks. But hard, steady shooting will run them off in a day or two, just as it will in a feeding field. Doves seem to prefer scummy, dirty-looking ponds and brackish water. Possibly the attraction of minerals in the water has some connection with their physiological needs in the production of "pigeon milk" for the young. But they do prefer clean, bare ground to land on and walk to the water. You will seldom if ever find them where the banks of a pond are grassy right to the water's edge. Where the water has receded or a pond has partially dried up, leaving a wide band of mud-flat around—that's a favorite drinking place for doves. If you find such a place and the doves are using it, you'll see small dove feathers that have collected around the edge of the water.

In the arid country of the Southwest, the area around a desert water tank is likely to provide good shooting. Both mourning doves and whitewings are attracted to water tanks, and I'm told that the high-flying whitewings tend to come down lower when heading toward water.

Shooting in the Rain: I suppose most dove hunters have been rained out a few times. Although dove shooting in the rain is not the most comfortable or productive kind of gunning, it can

Gunner picks up bird he dropped at edge of water as doves came in for last drink before going to roost.

be done. During a hard rain doves ordinarily cease flying, but if it is feeding time and the rain lets up somewhat they will fly again shortly. I've watched them fly in and out of feeding fields during a steady drizzle.

Identifying Doves: Hunters quickly learn to identify doves in flight. These birds never seem to rest their wings or dip like a blackbird or a woodpecker. It is always a steady, powerful, rhythmical wingbeat that carries the bird along at a rapid clip. The speed and agility of the species is always amazing to a new dove hunter, especially one who has observed the hesitant, timid movements of cooing doves nesting in a backyard. Migrating doves probably cruise along at 35 or 40 miles an hour, but when they're flaring from gunfire as they cross a field—and especially if they have the benefit of a tailwind—a lot of shooters claim the birds hit 70. And while the wingbeats are steady, the flight path is often erratic, twisting, evasive. Anyone who averages two doves for four shells is definitely a good wingshot.

A dove in flight appears gray or gray-brown on a bright day, but can look almost black in poor light, and the wings look darker than the body. The bird is much slimmer than a pigeon—more streamlined—with narrower wings that rake back more than a pigeon's and with a long, tapered tail

Most dove shooting is much like this—long passing shots as doves careen over wide-open feeding field.

rather than the pigeon's almost squared-off fan.

In some parts of the West a hunter can shoot mourning doves and whitewings both on the same day in the same area and in pretty much the same kind of habitat. The whitewing is a little plumper than a mourning dove and is easy to recognize by its big, white, sharply contrasting patches on the wing coverts and its shorter, blunter tail with broad white tipping at the corners. In flight it doesn't dip, rise and twist quite as erratically as a mourning dove but it provides tough shooting, all the same. Incidentally, whereas whitewings don't make any flight sound, Eastern shooters are famil-

112 · The Dove Shooter's Handbook

No one would have trouble identifying this dove by its white wing patches, white corners on wide tail.

iar with the soft whistle of air through a mourning dove's primaries when a bird flies close enough.

Hunting Pleasures and Esthetics: The pleasures of dove hunting are as hard to evaluate as the recreational and esthetic values that are not easily

Above: Man and boy wait at edge of sunflower patch.
Below: Good bet is in cornfield where silage is cut.

(if ever) figured into cost-benefit ratios for public works or private developments to "improve" man's living conditions. The way some of us see it, what is sometimes lost because of such a project is more valuable than the "improvements" resulting from it. How do you put a value on your feelings and appreciation for what comes naturally; that giddy-headed chest-button-popping syndrome resulting from a day outdoors?

What is it worth to you to take a shooting stand in a harvested grain field, along with several other dove hunters sharing the anticipation, excitement and colorful splendor of a clear fall day? Obviously there is much more for the taking than just the doves. I think that if all the hunter carries home is a bag limit—so many ounces of wild meat—then he's missed most of what a dove shoot is all about.

Neither the shooting nor the resultant bag is the full experience. Surely the hunter recalls just as vividly how he sat back in a fencerow and watched a hot-weather whirlwind spin across a field, picking up dust and cornstalk leaves and funneling the debris up into the sky, high above the field, then releasing the load to drift slowly back to the ground while another funnel starts up some distance away.

Sometimes, while waiting for doves to come

Part of enjoyment is just keeping low profile and waiting patiently for doves on warm fall morning.

in, your gaze becomes a sleepy glaze. Then, suddenly, through the mental fog, something crosses your line of sight. Instinctively you whip up your gun as your vision clears. It's then that you recognize the "something" as a swallow. Swallows do fly somewhat like doves. Or maybe you're fooled for a split second by an airplane way off on the horizon or a dragonfly close up. Or a killdeer or a butterfly or a nighthawk or a gnat. At one time or another you'll get a start from all of them.

Later in the evening, when the shooting has tapered off to an occasional boom, you might linger at your stand savoring the day's events. You sit looking up at pink-bottomed clouds and the deep blue sky and feel the first chill in the evening breeze after a hot day. A lone, last dove, finished feeding, picks up out of the field and comes winging over you. You don't move your gun, you just look. The up-slanting sun rays spotlight his buffy-gold breast and glisten off the underwings. You watch him out of sight; he's on his way to his favorite watering hole for the long evening drink and on to the roost. Silently staring after him, you wish him well. Peculiar, isn't it? After shooting at him and his kin all afternoon you have this special regard and admiration for the bird. A non-hunter would either find that hard to believe or would wonder about your emotional stability, to put it mildly. But if you're a hunter you know the feeling, and since you could never explain it to a non-hunter you keep it to yourself. Well, perhaps that's as it should be.

Guns, Shells and Shot: I guess just about every make and model of shotgun is used to hunt doves. Single-barrels, over-and-unders, doubles, automatics, pumps; 12 gauge, 28 gauge, 26-inch barrels to 32-inch barrels, open cylinders to full chokes—they all show up at the fencerows and water holes. All shot sizes are used, too, from No. 9

After connecting, shooter chambers two more loads of No. 8's in his improved and modified 12-gauge.

118 · *The Dove Shooter's Handbook*

Author's son holds up brace of mourning doves he bagged with his 20-gauge single-barreled shotgun.

skeet loads all the way to high-brass No. 4's.

One group of dove hunters I see regularly uses large shot in heavy loads with full-choke guns. These fellows are some sharp scattergunners. They load their own shells, practice their shooting the year around and get their share of whatever is in season, including doves. They claim the 4's and 5's and a 30-inch full choke increase the sport—"too easy to hit them with an open bore and No. 8's." Well, some would agree, others wouldn't. I feel that any way you can shoot your doves (legally) is a good way. The only thing I'll maintain is that you do have to hit them to bring them down and if you ever learn to place your No. 4's or whatever in their way, they will come down. These fellows shooting heavy loads and tight patterns don't have many cripples fly off, which sometimes happens with light loads of 8's and 9's. And when one of these specialists takes a stand where the birds are passing over high with a good tailwind, the shooting is something to watch.

Actually, any bore or shot size is fine, if you let the doves come into the range of your gun and loads. Shooting too soon, at birds too high or too far out, gets poor results. These are the shots that pick feathers and cause crippling losses.

Some shooters never seem to miss, others don't seem to be able to hit. There's a knack to wingshooting. Some learn it the first try, others have a hard time ever catching on. But it can be learned. All the stuff you read is a big help but only if you can practice. There are shooters, like myself, who have to learn over again every year. I know when I've got the swing down pat because I'll probably hit six or seven doves in a row. Then when I know all about it, maybe around the end of the season, I'll miss a dozen in a row. So, I just have to learn all over again the next year.

But why worry? Missing is part of the game. Perhaps you can salve your feelings with the knowledge that a clean miss is as good as a hit in some ways; hits and misses contribute the same amount to the game-management fund. Anyway, where else can you try all types of wingshooting, all types of shotguns, all types of shot and shells — in a single afternoon?

Probably No. 7½'s and 8's are most often used since small shot provides thicker pattern. Some hunters use field loads while others say they prefer high-velocity stuff late in the season, when birds have learned to fly high and flare promptly at the sound of gunfire. The most popular guns are 12 and 20 gauge, bored improved or modified. The birds may look small and fragile, but I'm told that for doves the 12 gauge continues to outsell any other bore size, North or South, East or West.

It's really something to see a shooter powder a dove barreling along downwind, slightly bending the sonic barrier. Of course, it's even better if you powder the dove yourself. Wild-flying doves with a good stiff wind helping them along are aptly called "gray bullets." There are many guesses around as to how fast a dove flies: "They loaf along at 30 miles an hour." "They cruise at 40." "They may attain 70 miles an hour in full flight." Well, I don't know how fast they can fly. I know I've driven alongside a dove for three-quarters of a mile or so with the speedometer steady on at 40, and the dove didn't appear to be laboring. A leisurely cruise like that is one thing; flying through a cordon of hunters with a 20-mile tail wind and making a power dive—that's flying! I recall shooting at a dove once about 30 yards up and I hit his next of kin about 20 yards behind him. I can't compute his exact speed from those figures, but I guess he

Ejected shell flies as shooter tries again. Pumps and autos are popular for pass shooting at doves.

122 · *The Dove Shooter's Handbook*

All those empty hulls don't mean hunter limited out; he's gone back to his car for more shells.

might have been going 50 miles an hour. Which brings up the question of how to hit a dove.

Shooting Technique: How do you lead doves? That's as good a question as the one about barrel length or shot size. The old-time dove shooters who say "swing and follow through" are the most consistent hitters I've watched. So if you can learn that technique, stick to it. A snap-shooter is good, I've noticed, if he doesn't see the dove coming. That way he doesn't have time to get jerky and miss. You can also help your hitting average somewhat if you'll carefully select the spots from which you shoot.

Field Position: Before you take the field to shoot, if you can restrain yourself, watch the doves flying for a few minutes. Usually they'll follow a path if they're going on through. In a field they are using, pick a spot with the sun at your back, under a tree or in a fencerow. A depression in a hill, just below the crest, is a good spot. But don't hide so well you can't see to shoot. Once you get into position, sit still. Most doves won't notice you if you don't move. Then estimate your effective killing distance and keep your shots within this distance. If you don't get the hang of it quickly, don't let it worry you. The "experts" who tell you how don't always hit them either. But if it bothers you and you just have to get some doves—well, remember that fencerow and that 20-mile wind? Get on the other side and take the doves coming upwind! Sometimes they'll hang there in the wind while you reload.

Effects of Hunting Pressure: Gun pressure is very heavy during the first part of the season. About 60 to 70 percent of the doves taken may be killed within the first 10 days; many of these birds are bagged the first weekend. There is, of course, a lot of good shooting to be had later on but fewer hunters are out then. The early hunting pressure causes doves to change. They become wary, their flight becomes fast, choppy, erratic. They will be

Hunter has almost limited out by quitting time; generous bag limits reflect abundance of doves.

diving and climbing, boring through the air with none of the loafing along you see during the opening days. A couple days of shooting will sometimes cause doves to abandon a feeding field or a water hole they've been using for weeks. Heavy shooting pressure in the more northerly range can start them on their migration out of the area. I recall a roost shoot at an Osage orange hedgerow where the doves came in later and later each evening because of the shooting at the site. After the fourth evening, they waited until it was so dark you couldn't tell a dove from a robin. They came in low, not against the sky, and flipped up into the trees at the last split second. And in a short time they abandoned the roost altogether.

Doves are especially spooky late in the season. After they have been subjected to hunting pressure for a month or more, pass-shooting may be all you can expect. At this time, a flock feeding regularly in a particular field will sometimes leave after only a single shot and not return. You can, however, get some fine pass-shooting if you station yourself on their flyway going to the feeding field, and take care not to turn them away en route.

You may wonder why doves sometimes seem to disappear—literally vanish—after three or four days of heavy shooting. It's true that doves are gregarious, they like each other's company. But they don't *have* to flock up. After being shot at a while they seem to realize this. They begin to fly trick patterns and in general take better care of themselves. Staying alive is a full-time job then and only the extremely fast and wary will survive the winter. They stay in good cover until feeding time, then flip down into the nearest feeding field and fill their crops. Having fed, they'll pass quickly to a water hole and back to the roost. After mid-September, food is plentiful and they can feed anywhere. If they are not bothered at this time they may tend to build up into large flocks but, as

At top is typical commercial decoy; hunter at bottom has set decoys enticingly along fence.

With decoys in branches for long-range visibility, hunter places additional stick-ups at water's edge.

mentioned above, a single shot may spread them all over the countryside again.

Decoys and Calls: Decoys do work. Years ago, when I first heard about dove decoys, I didn't see much point in trying to decoy birds that just naturally drifted in over the shooters anyway. In most situations, maybe it is unnecessary work. But if you want to get by yourself, away from the crowded field, or pull doves in off a flyway or make them circle your end of a field or pond, then get some decoys. They work well in trees, on a fence or on the ground, depending on how you want to shoot. Often decoys will bring you birds that would otherwise stay away, and in the late season they're much more valuable. You can use silhouettes or blocks; both are effective.

Another thing to bear in mind is the "whistling wings." Whistling to imitate the sound of dove wings also attracts flying doves. It doesn't seem to make much difference early in the fall but later, during the winter season, I've seen it work with high-flyers passing over.

As for dove calls, I've never used them or seen them used very often. Because few doves are still calling during the hunting season, a call seems out of place and I don't have much faith in its ability to attract doves into shooting range. But then, admittedly, I was skeptical about decoys at one time, too, so don't take this as the final word on the subject. Perhaps, in your region, calling may be worth a try.

Camouflage: Hunters usually wear something drab — army color or dark green or any dark hue. The use of camouflage hats, suits, jackets and netting is ideal. Netting material is now being made up into jackets more and more. It lets some air through to the skin and a September afternoon can be a real scorcher. At any type of shoot, dark clothes or at least a camouflage jacket will be of help.

Last year I saw a dove hunter on his stand in the middle of a field with a shocking-scarlet deer-hunting outfit. I guess he didn't know that doves, like many birds and unlike most mammals, can see color clearly, and they have sharp eyesight. But on the other hand, maybe that hunter knew something I didn't. I believe he killed some doves.

With or without camouflage, it helps to stay low or in the shadows, or break your outline against a tree, bush, hedge, fencerow, the bank of an irrigation ditch or whatever you can find at a good shooting spot. Few dove hunters go to the extreme of camouflaging their guns as some duck hunters do, but it makes sense to keep a gun down out of the sun when not shooting.

Walking Them Up: Sometimes in mid-afternoon when the shooting slows and doves seem to have evaded the usual feeding area where you are, then you can try walking them up. Jump-shooting doves is not like the fast pass-shooting, but the birds do flush wild and make for sporty shooting this way, too.

You'll usually find them working in a field of standing corn, beans, sorghum grain or such. Then again they may use a wheat-stubble or weed field. You might also flush them in a woodlot or thicket. The main thing to remember is that the cover is continuous and sometimes quite thick. In fact, the cover may be tall enough to limit your vision and thick enough to make your downed birds hard to find. Hunt and pick them up one at a time. This is one case where you really need a retriever.

The well-known hunting writer Charles F. Waterman has tried to use pointing dogs (as I suppose others have at one time or another) on both mourning doves and whitewings; but his conclusion was that "doves seldom play that game satisfactorily." He was right—they certainly don't. But retrieving is another matter. Naturally, when I make suggestions of this kind I'm thinking primarily of the mourning-dove regions that I know best, but I'm told it's pretty much the same everywhere in the country and whether you're shooting mourning doves or whitewings. A good dog can save you

Without retriever, shooter might have lost this dove in thick ground cover. Dogs of many breeds are used.

downed birds that you wouldn't otherwise be able to find.

And there's one other thing to bear in mind about walking up doves: You must be careful not to trample a farmer's crop.

Retrievers: Dogs work well with doves if you'll take the precaution to keep them cool and well watered, especially the long-haired breeds. Labradors readily retrieve doves. All bird-dog types do, though some owners claim their dogs can't stand the feathers. Dove feathers do come out very easily, so dogs often get a mouthful when picking up a dove and then have trouble getting them all spit out. Some dogs won't fetch other game than the type they are trained on, and there are dogs, with and without pedigrees, that simply refuse to pick up a dove. I guess only the dogs know why this is so. But I think it's safe to say that most dogs that retrieve will retrieve doves. Try it next time.

I've seen many kinds of dogs used to fetch doves, from a beagle hound to a fancied-up, snow-white, perfumed poodle with a red ribbon around its neck. The owner said he was airing his wife's dog once and stopped to watch some shooting and "that damn pooch brought me this dove. Thought it was his toy, I guess." So after that he took the poodle hunting with him. He said the other hunt-

Dove Shooting · 133

Lab delivers mourning dove to hand after swimming out into farm pond to fetch it.

ers didn't mind a white poodle bouncing around picking up everybody's doves but they did think he ought to get rid of that red ribbon.

A big shoot can be rough on a dog, what with so much shooting and so many doves falling around him. A retriever is apt to get excited in these circumstances, but if he's kept cool and under a reasonable degree of control, with enough rest and water, it won't hurt him—provided, of course, that he's in good condition to begin with. Dogs save lots of doves, and they ought to be used more. But dogs can't count, so they need a little help from the gunners.

I recall a story about Ol' Blue, a big Labrador. His owner, Jack, was a very good shot with doves; always got his limit. Jack and Blue were at their stand in a fencerow when a wildlife officer drove up. As the officer got out of his car, Jack went to meet him.

"Got my limit, you wanna check me?"

"Yeah, let's see what you got."

The limit was 12 that year. The officer emptied the game bag and rapidly counted . . . "10, 11, 12—right. You've had a good day."

Just about that time they noticed Blue coming back from the fencerow with another dove in his mouth.

"Ha! Musta found one someone else

knocked down and couldn't find. He's great, Ol' Blue is, don't miss many. Hellova good nose. Good boy, Blue!"

While they watched, Blue dropped the dove at his owner's feet and without waiting turned and ambled back toward the fencerow again.

"That'll do now, Blue. We gotta go now. C'mon, 'at's a good boy."

But Ol' Blue just kept working on up the fencerow.

"That's *enough*, Blue, Boy! C'mere, Boy! *Come back here!*" Jack screamed, "Damn you, Blue!" as the officer grinned and followed the dog for a look at the extra doves piled in the fencerow.

4
Doves on the Table

Field Care

Some hunters dress their doves on the spot, or at least eviscerate them before leaving the field. In the case of a badly gut-shot bird this can prevent the edible portions from being soured by the contents of the entrails, digestive juices and so on. The primary purpose of on-the-spot dressing or drawing is to promote cooling of the meat. How important it is depends on several factors—how hot the day is, how cool you can keep your birds without cleaning them, how much time will elapse before you can get them home.

If you do clean them at your shooting station, bear in mind that no farmer wants the entrails left to stink in his fields, and neither do your fellow hunters who may be shooting from the same spot after you. Thoughtless hunters harm their own sport and wear out their welcome fast. You can car-

Dog has delivered dove in fine shape, and hunter can keep it that way by drawing it quickly or at least keeping it cool.

ry the cleanings away in a plastic bag or some other receptacle.

Just *don't* make the fairly common mistake of putting the birds themselves or the dressed meat in a plastic bag or an airtight game bag. Doing so produces a greenhouse effect, cutting off air circulation, intensifying the heat and holding moisture in. This combination, plus a shot-punctured crop or intestine, can start a bird "marinating in manure," as one of my colleagues vividly describes it, and a dove then gets overly ripe in a big hurry.

Naturally, such doves are unwelcome in the kitchen. A dove that has been given proper care in the field and on the way home, on the other hand, provides rich but delicate meat that is delicious. It's dark meat, like that of other migratory species. Darkness is a matter of rich blood supply carried through the tissues, and it characterizes birds that have to fly far and hard. I'm told that some of the uninitiated fear such meat will be coarse and too heavily flavored. If that were so, squab (and duck, for that matter) would not have been considered a gourmet's delight since at least the time of the Pharaohs and the very food-conscious ancient Romans. And well-fixed dove is still a treat.

Lots of hunters leave the legs, heads and feathers on their birds until they get home but do eviscerate their doves immediately. It's easily done by making a cut back of the point of the breast and pulling out the entrails. Some shooters use a small bird-hunter's knife—the kind that features a gut hook. But most hunters do it just about as quickly and neatly with their fingers. You can get your doves home in fine eating condition without cleaning them, but only if you can keep them reasonably cool and don't have days of travel before reaching home. I'm sure any hunter would kick up a giant fuss if his wife bought a chicken at the supermarket around noontime and tossed it in the car trunk to soak up 100° heat for two or three hours while she finished shopping and visiting and had her hair done. And the supermarket chicken, after all, has at least been cleaned and chilled, so it will take some time to go bad. Yet there are sportsmen who handle their game even more thoughtlessly. The doves they've bagged still retain their body heat, and some of them may be gut-shot. To pile them in the sun or in a hot car trunk will ruin them almost as fast as sealing them up in a plastic bag.

Whether or not you dress them in the field, keep them in the shade—or better, still, in a cooler on ice, but not in ice-water. When you see a courtly old gentleman sitting comfortably in the shade of a fencerow, relaxing on a folding stool, with a gun across his lap, a shell bag or box on one side of him and a cooler on the other, you're probably looking at a Southern dove shooter of the old school; he's been at it for quite a while and he knows what he's doing. The faster your birds cool, the better they'll keep. If you have no cooler, spread them out in the shade, at least, and carry them away in a paper bag or some other sack that permits ventilation. Even cleaned birds can be taken home safely in a paper bag, but don't wash them in the field unless you can keep them in a cooler or on ice. Water removes the natural protection against the bacteria that cause meat to "ripen" quickly. Just the simple precautions I've described will pay big dividends at eating time.

Cleaning and Cooking

Shucking the Breast Only: Since a dove is a small bird and the main eating portion consists of the breast, many hunters save work by simply shucking out the breast and not bothering with the rest. That way, it isn't even necessary to eviscerate your game. Start by cutting off the wings and head. Then hold the dove in both hands, breast up. Put your thumbs together along the keel—the point of the breast—and press down and away. The skin (feathers and all) will easily separate, exposing the breast muscles.

Now all you have to do is push the skin

down to the wing joints, hook a thumb under the rear point of the breast and pry it up and out. (Some old-timers have a knack of pulling the breast off without even cutting away head or wings.) A few feathers will probably remain sticking on the meat. Pick them off and you're finished.

Dressing a Whole Bird: There are a few hunters who simply eviscerate and skin all their game birds because they feel that plucking is too much trouble. But the feathers come off a dove

Doves have been kept on ice in bucket until end of hunt, and now gunners can clean them all at once.

very easily, and many hunters feel that doves are tastier when all the skin (and fat beneath it) is kept intact. Aside from the fact that this helps to keep the meat juicy, the skin itself tastes good. Just pick off the feathers, they come off easily. Finish by rubbing away the small ones with your fingers.

To use the whole bird instead of just the breast meat, remove the head, feet and small outer wing sections (which have little meat and are easily taken off at the outer joint). Now hold the bird breast down in one hand, put the point of the knife next to the neck, and split the back open to the tail so that the entrails can be quickly drawn out.

Preparing Doves for the Table: According to one school of thought, the heart, liver and possibly the gizzard of even such small birds as doves should be saved, and there are recipes that call for giblets though I doubt that most hunters bother. According to another school, doves should be soaked overnight in a light marinade or at least in cold, lightly salted water for a few hours, with or without a little vinegar; again, I doubt that many people bother, because doves are usually tender and savory and need no such special treatment. According to some cookbooks, one whole dove per person is sufficient; anyone with a normal appetite is likely to want three or more.

When small birds are cooked in a Dutch

Doves on the Table · 143

oven or casserole, they're usually done gently, slowly, over low heat. Some cookbooks recommend low heat both for roasting and for other methods of preparation, but others insist on the importance of preheating the oven for small birds so that the meat is subjected only to a brief cooking but with plenty of heat.

Bear in mind that wild birds are much lean-

After gentle simmering in Dutch oven, braised doves are among most delicious of game birds.

er than domestic fowl. You may want to baste them liberally and often, or put a few thin strips of fatty bacon or pieces of salt pork on the breasts and legs. If you roast doves on a spit, it's a good idea to cover the meat for the first few minutes to keep it from hardening and drying out. Moist green cornhusks are sometimes used for the covering, as are bacon strips and even grape leaves. Foil is not recommended for spit-roasting, but for conventional oven roasting or baking you can put the meat in foil or in one of the relatively new "browning bags" available in markets.

Doves can also be stewed, braised, deep-fried or pied, and there are recipes calling for all sorts of wine sauces, cream sauces, cheese sauces and so on, although the meat is succulent and finely flavored without any sauce at all. As a matter of fact, if time is too short to follow a recipe or if you have some left-over doves, the meat can be made into a very tasty substitute for chicken in chow mein or for tuna in a salad. There are many other fine recipes, and instructions in many good cookbooks—for example, *Cooking Over Coals*, by Mel Marshall, published by Winchester Press in 1971; *How to Cook His Goose (and Other Wild Games)*, by Karen Green and Betty Black, published by Winchester Press in 1973; and *The Outdoor Cook's Bible*, by Joseph D. Bates, Jr., published by Doubleday back in 1963 and still in print.

In hunting books concerned with one particular kind of game, I've noticed that the author frequently lists a few favorite recipes which make him appear to be something of a gourmet cook. Rest assured here and now that the description doesn't apply to me. I use up all my ability getting doves down on the ground and ready for the pot; then there's a gap in time and activity before I can give them further attention at the table.

But I surely wouldn't want to disappoint anyone who expects to find recipes here. So I did a little research and questioning and came up with some cookbook and hand-me-down recipes that should please most everyone. The quantities are supposed to be for one generous serving. However, you can vary the proportions to suit yourself.

Deep-Fried Doves

4 whole doves (quartered) or 6 dove breasts
peanut oil or other cooking oil
½ cup milk
½ cup flour
salt and pepper to taste
1 tablespoon butter
½ tablespoon flour
½ cup heavy cream

<u>Directions</u>: In a deep skillet, bring about 2-inch depth of cooking oil to high heat. Dip meat in milk, then roll it in flour seasoned with salt and

pepper. Drop pieces into hot oil, only a couple at a time so that heat is not lowered and skillet is not crowded. Brown for 3 or 4 minutes, turning frequently, then drain birds on paper towels or cloth and pour off oil but do not wipe pan. If you use giblets, chop them and place them in skillet on low heat; with or without giblets, put in butter, let it begin to brown and sprinkle it with $\frac{1}{2}$ tablespoon flour. Slowly add enough cream and left-over milk to form smooth gravy. Do not let mixture boil. Stir away any lumps, then put doves back in pan with gravy just long enough to reheat.

Doves Arkansas

4 whole doves (quartered) or 6 dove breasts
cup flour
$\frac{1}{2}$ teaspoon ground
$\frac{1}{2}$ peppercorns
$\frac{1}{2}$ teaspoon paprika
salt to taste
$\frac{2}{3}$ cup bacon drippings
1 tablespoon butter
$\frac{2}{3}$ cup dry white wine

<u>Directions</u>: Roll meat in flour seasoned with pepper, paprika and salt. Brown in bacon drippings, then drain meat and pour off drippings but do not wipe skillet. Return meat to skillet, add butter and wine, simmer gently for 10 minutes. (Some people prefer pressure cooker to skillet; in this case, set control to 10 pounds, cook for several minutes at 325°, then for 10 minutes at 220°.)

Roast Doves with Grapes and Wine

4 whole doves (plucked, drawn, but not split)
1 medium-size mild onion, thinly sliced
1 cup white seedless grapes
salt and pepper to taste
$\frac{2}{3}$ cup butter or bacon drippings
$\frac{1}{4}$ cup melted butter
$\frac{1}{3}$ cup sauterne
$\frac{1}{2}$ cup chicken broth

Directions: Stuff doves with onion slices and grapes, then close them up with small skewers. (Stuffing tends to spill out of small birds; if you wish, cover openings with short bacon strips pinned by skewers.) Sprinkle birds with salt and pepper, and brown them lightly in butter or bacon drippings. Make basting liquid by combining melted butter, wine and broth. Brush birds with liquid. In baking dish, roast for 30 to 40 minutes in 350° oven, basting frequently.

Broiled Doves, Marinated

4 whole doves (split or quartered) or 6 dove breasts
$\frac{1}{4}$ cup sugar
$\frac{1}{2}$ cup soy sauce
1 garlic clove, crushed

Directions: Marinate birds for 3 hours in mixture of soy sauce, sugar and crushed garlic, then broil (preferably over coals) until tender. Baste with marinating liquid. Meat is done when leg bones can be twisted away easily, or when breast meat feels tender as you probe it with a fork.

Turtled Doves

4 whole doves (quartered) or 6 dove breasts
½ cup flour
salt and pepper to taste
⅔ cup butter
½ can turtle soup
3 strips lean bacon

Directions: Roll meat in flour seasoned with salt and pepper, then brown lightly in butter. Drain meat. Place in casserole with bacon strips and turtle soup. Simmer gently for 30 minutes.

Sautéed Doves with Chestnut-Mushroom Sauce

4 whole doves (split) or 6 dove breasts
½ cup butter
1 tablespoon bacon drippings
2 small, mild onions, chopped
salt and pepper to taste
2 dozen small to medium chestnuts, roasted, peeled and cut in small chunks
½ cup red or white drinking wine (California Burgundy recommended)
5 ounces canned (cooked) mushroom buttons or pieces in their juice (not drained)

Directions: Melt butter and bacon drippings in skillet. Add chopped onions and let them just begin to brown. Add doves, salt and pepper. Sauté slowly, over low flame, for 7 or 8 minutes. Turn meat, add chestnuts, sauté for another couple of minutes. Add wine, mushrooms, mushroom juice; cover and continue low heat for 8 to 10 minutes.

5
Regulations, The Dove Harvest and the Importance of Hunting

Regulations

For many years, the previously mentioned 1918 Migratory Bird Treaty between the United States and Britain was our only international agreement for the conservation of migrating species. However, doves and many other birds not only cross our upper border into Canada but also our lower border into Mexico. Mourning doves are found that far south (and even farther) and a much greater percentage of whitewings apparently winter below the border—through Mexico and clear into South America. A second protective treaty was therefore enacted in 1937 between the United States and Mexico. It's probably safe to say that the two treaties, plus additional legislation based on them, have been instrumental in conserving doves and other migrants, including both game and nongame species.

Shooters greet first flights
in shirtsleeves weather that typifies
early part of dove seasons.

At the time of the first federal controls, only 22 states permitted dove shooting, but the populations of these birds have fared well since then, and at this writing 31 of our mainland states have legal dove shooting while open seasons are being considered in still more states. In addition, a closely related species called the Zenaida dove can be hunted in the Virgin Islands; Puerto Rico has a season on the Zenaida as well as the mourning dove and whitewing dove; and Hawaii has a season on the mourning dove, laceneck dove and barred dove. (Those last two are exotic varieties, introduced to Hawaii and native to Asia and Malaysia, respectively.)

Setting Shooting Dates: Every year in June the U.S. Fish and Wildlife Service consults the experts from various state game and fish agencies, private agencies and organizations and institutions, then determines a season framework which shows the broad outside limits and restrictions that will be applied to dove hunting that year. Any state may then have an open season on doves, but the state must fit its regulations within the federal framework. For example, the framework might allow a 12-dove bag limit and a 70-day season between September 1 and January 31. A state may further restrict but never extend those limits. Other restrictions apply to such matters as daily shooting hours, type of gun, shell capacity, split seasons, zoning and the prohibition of baiting.

The regulations are published each year in June and copies may be obtained from federal or state Fish and Wildlife Officers or at their headquarters or at a post office. Sometimes the regulations take quite a while to be circulated, but they should always be available in advance of the hunting season.

State game departments must cautiously watch the framework with an eye toward further restrictions. In many states, especially those having a September season, the harvest is composed largely of locally produced doves. These population segments may need added protection if hit by disease or other hardships, to assure survival of adequate breeding populations for the next year.

Regulations can and do effectively control the kill. The opening dates are quite important for migratory species. In the North and Central states, doves begin to move rapidly after the middle of September. Delaying the opening date for two weeks could greatly cut the total kill. Some other factors may enter into decisions about the opening and closing dates. For example, people have asked why the season doesn't open in August, if that's when the population reaches a peak. Theoretically, the time to harvest doves is at the peak. But

To avoid loss of hard-to-find kills, gunner stops to look for his bird and add it to pile after each shot.

we can't know in advance exactly when the population will peak. That becomes known only when it actually occurs and the next census shows a decline. (See census graph, Chapter 6, illustrating dynamics of annual dove populations.) Furthermore, some doves might still be nesting in August. Some local areas might be better off shooting in February when large flocks of migrant doves collect there. But that is too near the nesting season. Another very good reason is that the Federal dove regulations set the opening date as September 1 and closing date as January 31, and game officials prefer not to request any alteration of this agreement for fear that one change would lead to another and in the long run could cripple the Treaty.

From the ratification of the Treaty until the late 1950's, dove regulations were essentially restrictions, and the official attitude toward the dove hunter bordered on persecution each time he took the field. Baiting laws were arbitrary, ambiguous, outrageous and ridiculous. Definitions of right and wrong were left to the discretion of the wildlife officer, who did his level best to try to figure out what the law meant for him to do. Many borderline cases were brought into court and the "violator," faced with the alternative of going to the federal court, often pleaded guilty to an offense he didn't know or didn't feel he had committed. I recall one case in which an officer looked over the grounds and gave his verbal approval to the landowner and the shooters. Later on that afternoon, another officer came by and arrested them for shooting over an illegal field. Both officers had read the same laws but interpreted them differently.

In the long decade from the late 1940's to the late 1950's many distinct changes were made. With more and better dove-population and life-history data being obtained and studied, serious questions were explored as to the need for such strict regulations. Many individuals working on doves across the U.S. pooled their data to get better answers about regulations. From tests of specific regulations, the factual data gathered by the cooperators in the Southeastern Dove Study were, to my knowledge, the greatest single factor in bringing about more reasonable and equitable rules for dove shooting. We still continue to benefit from the much-tested and subsequently modified rules applied to baiting, zoning, split seasons and bag limits. No less important was a new law under the heading of "Wanton Waste," making it legally mandatory to make a reasonable effort to retrieve downed doves. All this has improved the hunting picture and made the sport more enjoyable to all.

As might be expected, since the work was concentrated in the Eastern Management Unit, the changes in the laws were most notable there and particularly in the Southeastern states. However, the more general aspects are enjoyed nationwide. That is to say, while specific regulations may differ from one Management Unit to another, based on production and harvest estimates, the overall hunting regulations and framework are more equitable throughout the dove-hunting states. Whitewing shooting as well could benefit by the general rules applied to mourning-dove shooting, but a hunter can expect separate and immediate restrictions where warranted.

Present Regulations: All states that permit dove shooting have biologists on the game-department staff to study dove movements and provide management recommendations. They know the best times for open seasons and they select opening dates that provide the most opportunity for the dove shooter while affording most adequate protection for the doves. The hunter must compromise and in some instances forego a larger bag limit for the well-being of the bird.

As biologists have learned more of the life history of doves, and game departments have conducted studies of actual dove shooting, the regulations have been gradually modified. The most lib-

Field of corn being cut for silage is legal shoot

eral rules were set in 1969 and 1970, in the states of the Eastern Management Unit, with a bag limit of 18 doves and a 70-day season. The framework of federal regulations may vary in the three units, depending on the data gathered in each of them. In the 1973 season the regulations for the Eastern Management Unit again took the bag limit back to 12 doves, as this was considered about right for a reasonable harvest.

Even more important than the modification of limits has been the much more reasonable inter-

if corn has not been dumped there to bait birds.

pretation of just what constituted baiting and illegal shooting areas. The limits and number of shooting days have had to be reduced a bit, but the sensible baiting regulations continue. As a result of further studies and data analyses, there has been a change in dove food-plot management in that a field of grain planted for doves may now be legally manipulated. Under the heading of "Baiting Section," the rules now state that "nothing in this paragraph shall prohibit [taking doves] on or over any lands where shelled, shucked or unshucked corn, wheat

Under current regulations, crops such as brown-top millet can be grown specifically to attract doves.

or other grain, salt, or other feed has been distributed or scattered as the result of bona fide agricultural operations or procedures, or as a result of manipulation of a crop or other feed on the land where grown for wildlife management purposes: Provided, that manipulation for wildlife management purposes does not include the distributing or scattering of grain or other feed once it has been removed from or stored on the field where grown."

So, as I read it, this means you can now grow anything in a field to attract doves, and then you can even cut it and rake it or run a bush-hog machine over it. Such growing and manipulation would all be legal. But you are not allowed to carry out grain or whatever from another place and dump it in a field to attract doves to shoot. One final note here about checking regulations of this kind: I've said it before and I'll say it again—doves are an annual crop, and each year's crop comes with its own set of rules and considerations as to hunting. Be sure to check the regulations each year before you go shooting!

Because of these reasonable interpretations, the hunter can now take the field without looking back over his shoulder and worrying whether some officer might arrest him for something he isn't aware of. And the officers are much more confident in carrying out their duties. With more and better effort to keep abreast of population dynamics, dove-hunting regulations are more wisely applied now. These regulations and their enforcement are the prime management tools.

Present dove regulations probably are about as liberal as most hunters would ask for, though some game-department personnel feel that even now a few of the restrictions are not technically justified—which means that there must be social factors influencing hunting rules. And so there are.

Even where the dove population might be able to withstand more gunning pressure, the hunter must compromise. The well-being of the species comes first. Such compromise is also an aid in persuading non-hunters that reasonable regulations are being formulated. Portions of our society are opposed to any hunting whatever, and wildlife ownership, remember, is vested in *all* the people. It is only through the willingness of both factions to compromise that a happy balance can be reached in dove hunting.

Present regulations seem to be pretty well accepted by everyone. For evidence of this we can point to the fact that violations of dove regulations (and resulting arrests) have dropped to a very low rate. I know two officers who checked over 500 hunters in the first two days of the 1971 season and found not one wrong-doer. That says a lot for the better, more understandable laws, better law enforcement and a willingness on the part of the hunter to take his fair share and leave the rest alone. The worst violation I generally see today is the failure to search adequately for downed birds. Occasionally one of the more exuberant shooters will pot-shot a killdeer or a robin or nighthawk or some other non-game bird, and maybe some fellow forgets to count and winds up with one or two more than the limit. But, as noted, these acts are not common and are frowned on among seasoned dove hunters.

Why No Rifles: I've been asked why you can't shoot doves with a .22 rifle. Well, it's my understanding that all migratory birds once came under the same set of regulations. Ball ammunition was prohibited because someone might shoot into flocks of ducks or geese when they raft up, and many could be crippled. Doves have now been separated from waterfowl in the regulations but the rule still applies to all migratory birds: You can't hunt them with a rifle. Several additional reasons have been given—that hunters would be tempted to shoot doves off powerlines, that they'd shoot off the powerline insulators, that ball ammunition (even rimfire .22 bullets) carry too far for safety in areas of human habitation or near fields where there are other hunters. Yet it's permissible to use a .22 for rabbits and squirrels, and even for quail or grouse! Why not for shooting doves out of a dead tree? Good question. It's one I don't have a good answer for.

Hunting Success and Data on Doves Bagged

Dove Popularity: Dove shooting at one time might have been called a rich man's sport since it was so demanding on the ammunition supply—and still is. No pot-hunter would have wasted his ammo to get a single dove at a time. Now with the whole country more affluent, people having more leisure and excitement so much in demand, dove hunting is attracting people from all walks of life. It is especially appealing to people in urban areas who may get away from work for a few hours of an

After successful dove shoot, hunters pose happily with wildlife officer who has checked their kills.

afternoon, and to people who like to get out and do a lot of shooting in a short time. Hardly any other shooting sport can provide as much action in a given amount of time. As of now, in states where dove shooting is legal, perhaps 25 percent of the license buyers hunt doves. Dove hunting is increasing, both in numbers of hunters and in the areas hunted. The greatest rise is near cities and towns, which contribute the bulk of the dove hunters (and incidentally quite a few dove huntresses, too).

For an idea of how popular dove hunting may be in your state you might compare it with Kentucky, which is comparatively rural and forested. According to studies of hunter populations and species preference in this state, the dove ranks fifth as to the number of hunter trips and second in total units of game harvested. This means the dove is not far behind the squirrel, our most popular species, and ahead of rabbits and quail. You can see how high the dove might rank in a more industrially developed, more populous area.

Hunting Success: By adding up the figures from surveys and counts, we get a picture of the "average" dove hunter. He takes home five or six doves a day and hunts five or six times a season, for about 30 doves per year. A state with 50,000 dove shooters may harvest from one to one and a half million doves per season. Hunters I've checked

Spot-checking during hunting season in Kentucky, game biologist ages doves by examining primaries.

tell me they shoot about five boxes of shells per season to get their share of the doves. They score on maybe one dove out of four shots. On that basis you can fit yourself into the good, better or best category of shooters.

Age of Doves Bagged: The ratio runs about six to eight doves of the year out of every 10 doves bagged. To tell the old doves from the young ones, examine the wings for white tips on the primary coverts, as per the instructions in Chapter 2, page 40. Remember, the coverts are the short feathers that overlay the outermost long flight feathers. Those 10 outer primaries are molted from the inside out to the tip. The long feathers from the middle of the wing that curve back toward the body are the *secondary* flight feathers. All juvenile primary coverts are tipped with white. As the primary feathers and coverts are molted, the new feathers and coverts come in. (See *Table for Aging Juvenile Doves*, page 42.) These coverts are then all brown or gray, *without the white tip*. As long as even one white-tipped covert remains (the last one would be over the 10th, or outermost, primary) the dove is a juvenile. After this last covert feather is molted, they are all solid brown, gray, buff—or whatever color you prefer to call it—and you can't tell by looking whether the dove is a young of the year or several years old. (Except that few doves are very likely to be more than a year old.) This complete adult plumage is attained in about six months or a little less, so in the hunting season there are always some early-hatched birds of the year that will have finished their post-juvenile molt and are classed as adults.

Percentage of Breeding Doves Bagged: In examining the hunter kill in early September for a period of many years, it was found that about three out of 10 doves bagged were adults and perhaps three out of a hundred exhibited signs of breeding or possibly had young in the nest. Adults that are potential breeders are distinguished by their glandular crop. To examine for this glandular crop, pluck the feathers off and peel back the skin covering the crop. If the bird is not a potential breeder the entire crop will be a clear, transparent sac and you can see the swallowed seed through it. If it is a potential breeder, male or female, each side of the crop will be thickened and fatty-looking, with many folds. These are the "pigeon-milk" organs that turn the small seeds into a milky, curd-like substance that the young feed on. If you tear open a breeder's crop, you'll find white milky curds and small seeds on the inside of the folds of these glandular pockets.

Weight of Doves Bagged: How much does your dove weigh? Using a gram balance, biologists have found that doves taken early in September average about four ounces. At 460 grams to the pound—about 30 grams to the ounce—the typical young dove weighs 114 grams (3.8 ounces) while the average adult weighs 120.5 grams (4.0 ounces). In our study we found considerable overlap—heavy juveniles and light adults. The minimum weight for an adult was about 100 grams. The maximum weight for a young dove was about 150 grams. So you see, you can't tell old from young just by the size of the bird.

Lost and Crippled Doves: Not finding your dead birds or having birds you hit fly off beyond retrieving is sometimes unavoidable but is nevertheless a serious matter. In hunt after hunt, year after year, I've found that about one out of five (20 percent) of doves hit were never retrieved. There is an excellent law requiring an honest effort to retrieve downed birds in order to avoid wanton waste. This law must be respected by hunters and enforced by the officers. Here is another area in which the hunter can help his sport by taking stock of his own and his partners' shooting problems and habits. Look for your own downed birds, and help others look for theirs. It is a simple matter to avoid shooting doves where they are apt to fall into dense ground cover such as a standing crop of beans or alfalfa or a weed field or a bushy spot in a woodlot. Where there is some risk of losing a dove, it pays to shoot and retrieve one bird at a time. Mark it down and if you have no dog go directly to it without taking your eyes off the spot, pick it up, then return to your shooting stand. If you don't find it where you think it fell, hang your hat or handkerchief there and begin circling the spot. Your hat will keep you from losing your mark.

Sure, I'm sermonizing. And like the preacher who keeps repeating the same old sermon, I'll promise to deliver a new one just as soon as all the congregation starts practicing the old one.

Hunters' Behavior: A regard for the rights of others shouldn't have to be dictated by shooting regulations. There is something the hunters themselves are going to have to regulate, and pretty soon, if they want to keep the sport free of further restrictions. Potentially more damaging to the sport than violations of formal regulations is a disregard for other people's rights and property. It's especially puzzling that anyone can mistreat people who were nice enough to allow hunting on their land. When the last of the free-for-the-asking hunting area is gone, it won't have been the fault of the landowner. Some have gone beyond what could have been expected of them in allowing hunting privileges. Lots of land is still open but more is being closed every year. There will always be dove hunting—for a fee. A landowner can put up with considerable annoyance if he is being paid. The worse the behavior, the more he has to work— and the higher the fee. But I don't think hunting will be the same, for me anyway, when it's necessary to buy a ticket to get into every field.

Most hunters I've encountered have been true sportsmen—gentlemen—but think a minute and see if you can recall any of the following: field gates open, crops trampled or driven over, broken-down fences, shot sprinkling on a house or barn roof, litter, empty shells lying around, drink cans floating in a farm pond, spooked livestock racing from one end of a field to the other, a pile of dove feathers and cleanings along the farmhouse road. Though the officers try to discourage such boorishness, it is not their job to teach hunters to respect the land they hunt on. Dove hunters will have to police their own ranks and take a direct part in stopping this nonsense. The alternative is to look forward to losing more and more hunting places and privileges. Dove hunters can teach each other, but sometimes this learning comes pretty rough. I recall one man who was trying to straighten out another across the field from him. After about three shots whanged into the trees above him I heard him shout:

"Low bird—don't shoot them low birds!"

Bang! Whang, Bang, Whang!

"Hold it! DAMMIT, I SAID—and he threw up his gun—*Bang! Bang! Bang!*—"don't shoot them low birds!"

Shooting back is one way to teach a lesson, I suppose.

Even with the best of comrades, it pays to watch out at a dove shoot. It isn't unusual to be checking a shoot and suddenly have to take a bel-

Hunting chiefly on farmlands, devoted shooters like this man harvest 40 to 50 million doves every year.

ly-buster to get out of the line of flight of a low-flying bird. Once I was examining doves on the edge of a field when a low bird headed my way. I flopped down, put my clip board in front of my face, and stayed there a while after I heard shot whang over me and hit the trees in the fencerow behind me.

A youngster about 14 or so plopped down beside me and began asking questions about what I was doing. A few minutes later a dove flew by and in his great haste to shoot, the youngster grabbed his gun — finger around the trigger — and plowed a furrow in the ground a yard or so in front of our noses.

Maybe things would be a bit safer if all hunters, kids and adults alike, had to take a hunter's safety test before they get their first license. I'm happy to see more and more states adopting that rule. And while they're giving a safety course, they might add a lesson or two about respect for the land and leaving things as they're found.

The alternative, a loss of hunting privileges, won't help anyone. Doves will go to waste, millions of dollars will be lost to the economy, thousands of hours of healthful outdoor recreation will be lost and—no less important—that part of our most cherished freedoms will be gone.

Importance of Dove Hunting

How Hunting Affects the Dove: As a guard against extinction, nature has a way of stimulating reproduction in the face of severe hazards. Moreover, since it is an axiom that in nature only the fittest survive, all hazards tend to promote natural selection toward more nearly perfect, hazard-resisting specimens. Dove shooting constitutes an additional hazard, to be sure. But it is a hazard which has given us direct recreational and economic benefits while also inducing a natural improvement in the broodstock. Perhaps 40 million doves a year are taken by hunters—probably requiring four times as many taxable shells. You can be certain that a species which annually pours millions of dollars into Federal Aid to Wildlife Restoration will be safeguarded for the future.

The dove is faring well under hunting pressure. In a hunted species there is less stability, and greater adaptability. Physiologically and ecologically, hunted birds are in better condition for survival. You might compare the dove with the non-hunted species that are reported to be on the decline. Since they generate no expenditures on their own behalf, there is little money to pay out to learn the causes of their plight, and hence only limited attempts to protect them or provide for their welfare.

The dove has been regarded as a symbol of peace from biblical times. It should also be regarded as a symbol of prosperity. I'm sure you'll find that where economic development progresses, dove hunting increases. The dove is a real capitalist agent that generates private enterprise and therefore is a true public benefactor. It has a measurable value all its own and therefore it will be looked after as well as most wildlife species, better than some. So you can look for the dove to be around for a long time.

Value To Other Species: The dove provides

much more revenue for wildlife funds than is spent on its management, so it lends financial support to many other game and non-game species that need to be studied but generate less revenue. It might be well to keep in mind that the arms-and-ammunition taxes and the license fees are paid only by those who hunt. Those who don't shoot have contributed nothing. We also know that there are incidental management benefits for other species: Habitat improvement for doves means habitat improvement for other wildlife. In this manner the dove contributes much more to wildlife than the public is generally aware of.

This, too, is now being recognized by the people in general who cherish wildlife and the outdoors. They realize that funds spent for management of our game species have also been benefitting songbirds and other non-game wildlife species. Recently in several states various programs have been proposed or introduced to gain funds that are allocated to the game departments. These funds will help *all* wildlife and will also tend to balance the payments due and improve the relations between hunter and non-hunter. No other species I can think of—hunted or not—does more than the dove for the cause of all wildlife.

Value to the Economy: Let's assume that in your state a million doves are harvested each year.

(Many states take more, some less.) And each dove bagged requires an average of four shots (which is reasonable) at a dime a shot (which is cheap). This amounts to $400,000 in your state each year. In order to get $400,000 in interest at five percent per annum you would need to invest eight million dollars, right? So your state alone, harvesting just a million doves, has a dove population flying around that represents an investment of eight million dollars in shotgun shells alone. (You can slide this figure up or down according to your state's dove harvest and your own notions about the cost of shells; my figures are probably very conservative.)

There are fairly reliable estimates of 40 to 50 million doves harvested in the U.S. each year. So you can multiply the $400,000 by forty and arrive at a total of 16 million dollars worth of shells fired at doves each year in the U.S. A $16,000,000 cash return each year at five percent interest would require a capital investment of some *three hundred and twenty million dollars!* Now you can begin to see the real value of a dove and why such birds must be expertly managed. And that's not all, since you use more than just shells in a dove hunt. Add food, drink, clothing, gasoline, etc., and you'd show a billion or more dollars in value for the nation's dove population.

There is yet another value. Figuring one

ounce for each table-ready dove, there would be some 40 million ounces—nearly two and a half million pounds—of dove breast. Worth how much? Compare it with beef or fowl.

So you see it's not at all limited to fun and healthful outdoor exercise, which in itself would have the same value per hour of recreation as baseball or tennis. Doves and dove hunting involve all phases of management and production and distribution and payrolls and purchase of goods and meat on the table. . . . Well, I'll stop on the note that doves are our billion-dollar birds.

6
Dove Management

What is dove management, actually? It is: (1) organization of state and federal wildlife-management offices having jurisdiction over doves; (2) funds necessary to provide for the field and administrative functions; (3) studies and procedures for obtaining needed information; (4) compiling, analyzing and evaluating results of studies; and, last but certainly not least, (5) regulations for using the resource—devising suitable laws governing the harvest of the production surplus and protecting a population base.

Management, then, is essentially inventory, research, production, development, maintenance and use—the same as management of anything else (a factory, for instance, or a power plant). Except that it is made somewhat more complex by the task of dealing with a living product for which exact numbers are never known.

Mourning dove, though hardy, has
short life span; population is
not undermined by controlled hunting.

We must study the product, determine needs, develop necessary tools for taking inventory and for estimating income and expenditures. The tools must then be applied as required to maintain the numbers at a desirable use level. It could be defined in many ways, but when we speak of dove management we mean taking an annual harvest by hunting while at the same time looking out for the welfare of the species. Why? We are interested in managing the mourning dove, surely, because it is a living thing, a separate, distinct species that deserves to keep its rightful place on this planet—but also because it is a game bird, a great and valuable game bird, the most popular game bird in the U.S. There are perhaps 40 to 50 million doves taken by hunters each year, and this harvest has immense recreational, social and economic impact on our society. We've estimated (in Chapter 5) how valuable the dove is just from the standpoint of shotgun-shell sales alone—not to mention all the incidental costs and benefits.

From a practical standpoint, it is because the bird is so valuable to our society and to industry, as well as to the individual person's recreation and esthetics, that the dove must be managed. We should never allow it to be neglected, over-used or wasted. Some species may well be dwindling down to the point of no return. Endangered species, they're called. But how many of these endangered species can claim a multi-million-dollar niche in our national economy? Few ever have. You might think of a species or two, like the buffalo and the passenger pigeon, that were once of great economic value but were very nearly or actually wiped out. But bear in mind that those were the days of market shooting, and there was no management, and no regulations or controls. Hunters now provide a means for looking after their game animals. They finance game management. The dove may encounter its ups and downs in terms of population as a result of disease or other factors beyond man's control, but it should never disappear because of overharvest or neglect. But on the other hand, it will have to take its chances along with man, as man influences his own environment.

Organization

Federal Agencies: As the dove is a migratory bird, its management begins at the national level, as the overall responsibility of the federal government. The agency in charge is the Department of the Interior, Fish and Wildlife Service, Bureau of Sport Fisheries and Wildlife, Migratory Birds Sec-

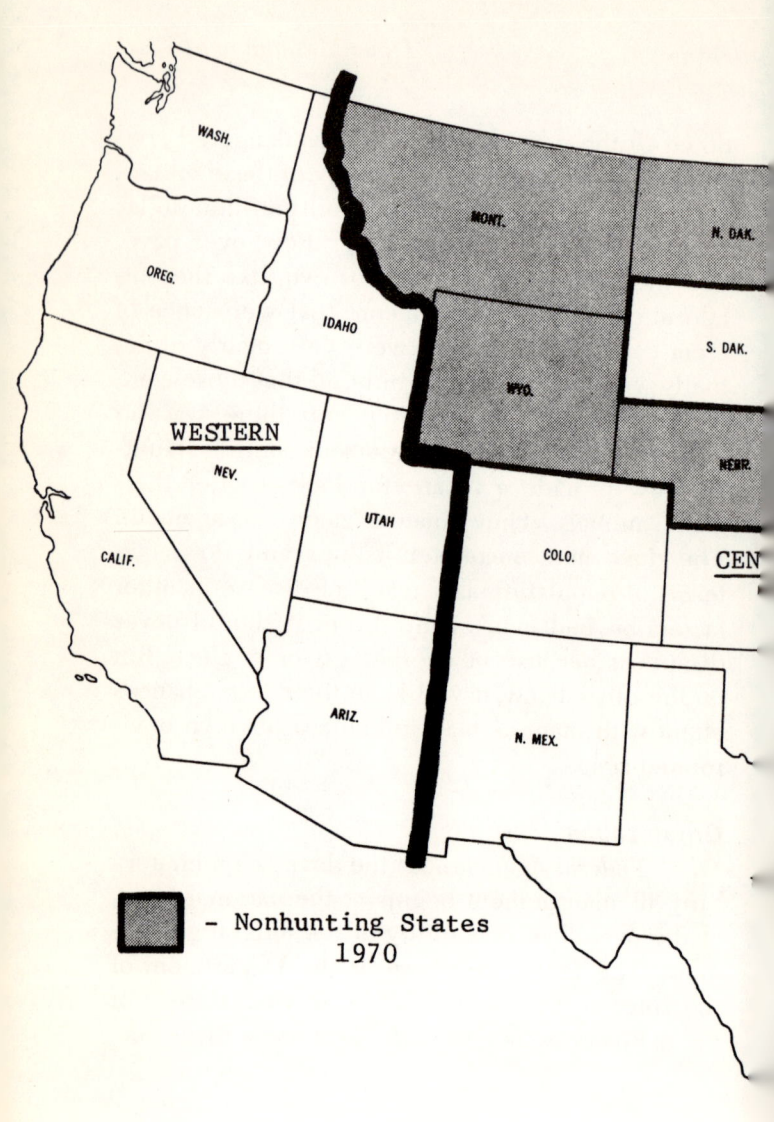

Mourning Dove Management Units

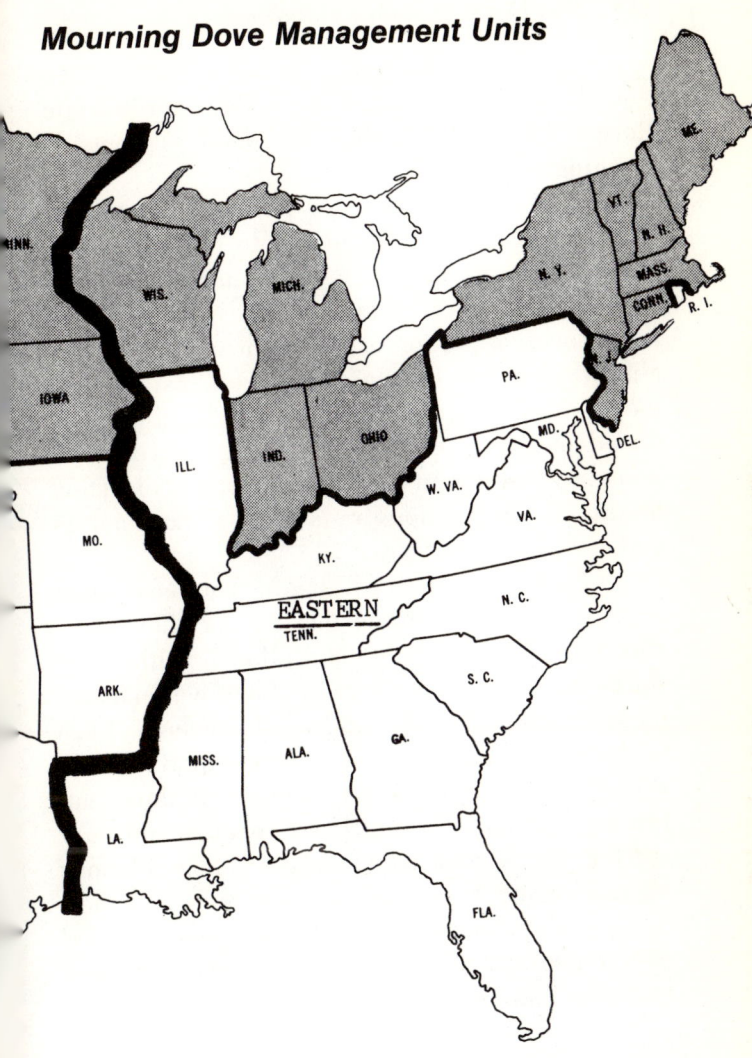

(After Bureau of Sport Fisheries and Wildlife Special Scientific Report Wildlife No. 158)

tion. This office is located at the Patuxent Wildlife Research Station at Laurel, Maryland, just outside Washington, D.C.

For purposes of dove management the 48 contiguous states are divided into three Management Units (see map). These are similar in function to the waterfowl flyways. Each of the three units covers a portion of the country that contains almost all of the known or expected dove movement within that unit. In other words, doves produced in any given state seldom go beyond the boundary of the unit in which that state is located. Studies and regulations are usually worked out on a Management Unit basis.

State Agencies: All states that have open seasons, as well as those that do not allow dove shooting — this decision is optional with each state — have the responsibility for dove management vested in their fish and wildlife agency. Each of these state agencies has a dove expert, or personnel assigned the species, to whom all dove matters are referred. These persons organize and carry out the state's dove work, make recommendations for management and harvest, and represent their agency at technical and regulatory meetings and conferences concerning doves. Two or more states' agencies finding similar situations may pool their information for regulation-study purposes. Several states within a unit may have common problems apart from those of other states in the same unit. In this case, they might conduct regional studies, then separate or pool the information for more efficient results and application of the findings. By the same token, a single state agency might further divide its area into sections to carry out more detailed studies of a smaller scope. Such matters as zone shooting or split-season shooting periods or area nest production may be important enough to a state to have these special divisions or studies.

Private Agencies: Private organizations and universities may have personnel conducting special studies separate from or in cooperation with the government agencies. These studies are usually to determine answers to a particular problem. It is not unusual to have representatives from private organizations sit in on meetings to determine whether proposed management measures are adequate and in keeping with their views of the needs for the species. These private agencies also represent non-hunting groups whose needs and desires are considered along with those of the hunters in forming the regulations.

Personnel and Administration: Whether with private, state or federal organizations or agencies, the dove-study personnel are technically schooled people with college degrees and years of experience in the wildlife field.

Besides studies to obtain technical information, there is also administrative management. After technical studies have been discussed and reported by representatives of state and federal agencies and special-interest groups such as the bird societies, these management administrators determine what would constitute an equitable harvest and set up the harvest regulations. After the federal framework for dove regulations is worked out and published, each state administrator then considers all the input and determines, within the framework, exactly what the opening and closing hours and dates and bag limits will be for the state's dove hunters.

Funds for Management

With all these studies—plus administration and such—somebody has to put up the money; there must be an income to pay for the research and the meetings and to publish the information. Where does it all come from?

State-Agency Funds: These funds are derived mostly from the Pittman-Robertson Wildlife Restoration Act, named after the two U.S. Congressmen who introduced and got the act passed.

The P.R. Act, as it's usually called, provides for an 11 percent excise tax on sporting arms and ammunition that is collected by the federal government and returned to the states. It is divided on the basis of the total land area and the number of licensed hunters in each state.

So, for each dollar you spend for guns and shells, 11 cents goes to wildlife management. This has been the main source of funds for most dove studies. Millions of dollars of P.R. funds have been spent on dove management over the past 30 years. The states must, however, match the P.R. money on a one-to-three basis. One dollar out of four is therefore state money and this comes mostly from license sales, the main source of revenue for most state wildlife agencies. Incidentally, the dove hunter is a big booster of the P.R. program because he shoots so doggone many shells (collectively, that is). Many dove hunters, many doves, many shots fired; the combination makes for many dollars in excise taxes collected. So much, in fact, that despite the large amount of money spent for managing doves (and this amount has dropped off drastically in recent years) more dove-generated funds are left over that go to the management of less popular game and also non-game species. The dove is, in spite of its small size, the real "big brother" financially to many wildlife species.

Private-Organization Funds: Agencies such as the Wildlife Management Institute, The Wildlife Federation, the Audubon Society and other organizations dealing with wildlife are, of course, privately endowed from grants, gifts and sales of their magazines and stamps and such. Private organizations have supplied considerable funds and study personnel to the cause of wildlife and wildlife studies. This is only a fraction, however, of the amount of money spent collectively by the hunters through their license fees and in the form of hunting-equipment taxes.

Federal-Agency Funds: The federal agency is funded by appropriations from Congress, in the same manner as any other federal agency. In addition to the general funds there have been specially earmarked monies granted by congress for specific dove studies. One grant is presently allotted to doves and other migratory birds, including woodcock, snipe, rails, coots and gallinules. Collectively these species are often referred to as the "webless migratory birds," to differentiate them from waterfowl, which are also included in the federal programs of migratory-bird management.

All sources of funds are important and all agencies work together to satisfy the hunter and to protect the dove. And just a brief addendum is in order here: Don't, because you are a hunter, listen to someone put down the "bird watcher," whatever the occasion. Birders have contributed a great deal, both in funds and real effort. They've also done much work in originating and carrying on studies that have had considerable impact on our wildlife-management programs. These V.I.P's certainly don't go out looking for recognition so I just thought I'd mention their importance to your sport. The list of literature in the back of this book includes many titles credited to them.

Other Funds: For the last 40 years the federal government has been raising extra money for wildfowl management by selling a Migratory Bird Hunting Stamp—generally called the Duck Stamp—which every duck or goose shooter must buy each season. There's nothing new about a similar fund-raising idea for doves, so I'll just mention that a dove-stamp bill is in the hopper as I write this. If it passes, then the dove hunter will be required to buy a special stamp, like the Duck Stamp.

I have my personal reservations about socking it to the dove hunter for more funds when *he is already contributing above what is being spent on doves*. It won't be much, aside from the inconvenience. The main justification will be to get a better idea of the number of known dove hunters and so a better estimate of the total kill—all of which tends to promote more efficient management. So, if things do go the stamp route, just put it down as another contribution by the dove—through the dove hunter—to less self-supporting wildlife species. It's a kind of bird "welfare" with the doves carrying the larger load. I'm sure you can find a parallel for this somewhere.

It is likely that such a dove stamp would be called a *Webless Migratory Bird Hunting Stamp*. Since the funds derived from it would benefit such species as woodcock, snipe, rails and gallinules, it is reasonable to assume that the stamp would also be required for hunting these birds. The stamp would be federally issued, like the Duck Stamp, and would be required in addition to a state hunting license.

Management Studies and Procedures

While employed by the Fish and Wildlife Service, Harold S. Peters compiled an interesting list of some 120 titles and authors of papers and reports on doves. They dated from 1873 to 1952. There were reports all along: 1888, 1909, 1918, 1921, 1925, 1928, 1933, 1938, 1940, 1945, 1946, 1950. Always, it seems, there was someone reporting his observations on doves. Not surprisingly, they reported some of the same findings that were reported in the extensive studies of the 1950's. The reports ranged from a single nesting observation to a number of detailed studies so highly valid and informative that, in fact, they laid the groundwork for the later studies.

In the late 1940's and early 1950's the dove gained immense popularity as a study object. Practically every college or university that had a wildlife school, and some that didn't, conducted a study on doves. Most were essentially life-history studies, with the conclusion that even though the dove is a very prolific, very adaptable, very desirable game bird, it was in need of protection. Such studies usually ended with recommendations for a hunting season (if hunting was to be permitted at all) beginning no earlier than October or November in order to allow nesting to be completed. Generally speaking, shooting doves was not looked on favorably by most early observers. This same type of thinking was apparent in the regulations from the time of the first dove laws in 1918 on up through the middle 1950's.

In the period from 1948 through 1956, the Southeastern States Cooperative Mourning Dove Investigations Study was conducted. There were three people working out of the Atlanta, Georgia, regional offices—George C. Moore and Harold S. Peters of the Fish and Wildlife Service and Leonard E. Foote of the Wildlife Management Institute—

who practically hand-hammered this cooperative venture into being and worked closely with the states to keep it functioning and headed in the intended direction. Life-history studies in the several states confirmed much of the early work. The main difference was that this cooperative dove study was management-oriented. All the findings and results were evaluated as to how best to manage the doves.

The earliest years of the cooperative study were used in laying the groundwork, developing management working tools. There was so much of a void that the accomplishments were many and the pace quite rapid; the catching up went in giant strides. At first, almost all information was new. In the middle 1950's, with other regions organizing dove-management study groups and committees, the basic knowledge became rather well established and accepted and the pace slowed. The refinements in information required more intensive study and more sophisticated procedures and often demanded specialized training. As it is commonly put, the specialists learned more and more about less and less. Today, after 25 years or so, we are still refining procedures and techniques and practicing dove management with the tools that were devised and found usable. It might be well to include a résumé of those tools. First, population measurements were a must, a way to tell what there was to work with—an inventory method. Census-taking procedures were devised, as outlined below.

Random Road Census: Based on some earlier work, a roadside census was set up and evaluated. This was a roadside count with the results expressed in numbers of doves per 100 miles. The figures, compared on a monthly and yearly basis, tended to show the monthly and annual population levels, the ups and downs. While such a count gave no actual total population estimates, it did show highs and lows—peaks and low periods in the states and in the region as a whole. It helped to establish periods of movements and relative nest success. A typical annual population fluctuation is shown in the accompanying graph. Peak population periods are now pretty well known, as is the time of movement. The nesting production begins to show up in the census in May, June, July and August and then the peak may be established when the next month's census (usually September outside of the Southern states) shows a decline.

This random census has been maintained in some states as a gauge on production levels in the late summer months. A one-time figure in itself can't tell much, but when it is compared with the figures of several years the population levels and trends can be noted and the deviations from the normal levels become evident.

Dynamics of Annual Dove Populations

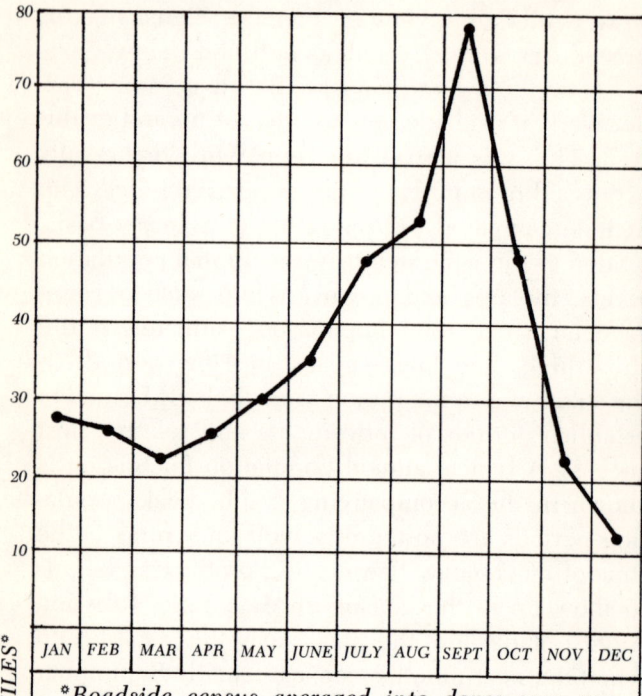

*Roadside census averaged into doves seen per 100 miles of travel. This shows when the breeding populations return and nest production increases. The population rises monthly to September, then as doves cease nesting and begin to migrate the population declines rapidly. This would be typical of mid-U.S. latitudes and most often for the more northerly states. For the Southern states, population peaks may be due to migrants coming in as the Northern populations decline.

Calling-Bird Census: Call Counts, or the Cooing Dove Census, is a procedure that was based on earlier studies. This count of the total doves heard calling has been the main survey tool for detecting annual ups and downs in the breeding population density and in the expected production peaks since the early 1950's. It is now conducted throughout the U.S. each year during May and June, when nesting is at its peak and the birds are all "at home" and least mobile. In all the U.S., there are approximately 800 census routes, each exactly 20 miles long. A given state may have 30 or more routes, depending on the amount of suitable nesting habitat. The routes are randomly selected so as to omit any bias or tendency of an operator to select a route in the best or poorest nesting territory. This random selection of study areas or routes helps to provide a more acceptable estimate of population status and trends. The routes are selected and mapped and the record forms prepared and mailed out each year by the Bureau of Sport Fisheries and Wildlife, Migratory Birds Section, from Washington, D.C., through regional offices. The field work is handled through the regional offices; usually the Federal Game Management Agent in each state processes the forms to and from the "cooperators." The cooperators, or census takers, are the federal agents themselves plus state wildlife biologists and conservation officers.

In conducting the count, an operator arrives at the start of his route ready to begin the count at exactly one half hour before sunrise. This is to include the time of the greatest calling activity—as those of you who have made some early-morning bird counts will recall. The operator gets out of his car to listen and count all calling doves for a period of three minutes, then proceeds rapidly to the next stop, and so on. Once the census is completed, a copy of the report is mailed directly to the Bureau in Washington, D.C., where tabulation and analysis begins. Copies are also sent to the state game agency and to the Regional Office, Branch of Game Management. The analyses of all route data by state and by Management Unit is completed and compared with the results of former years' data and population levels that are considered normal. Any statistically significant changes are noted. This census is the most important single indicator considered by the representatives of the regulations committee.

Weather conditions and other interference can influence the count. It often takes two or three tries to complete a 20-mile route count. What interference? You'd probably be surprised at all the racket that can go on at that time of the morning: cows bawling for their calves or for milking, dogs

Hunter bags single in area where birds have just moved in to escape severe weather farther north.

barking, frogs croaking—that's right, if you stop near a pond, several bullfrogs can virtually drown out every other sound. Then there are tractors starting up, people driving to work, roosters crowing. The best time to run a count is on a Sunday

In managed hunt area, doves are examined and wings are collected for study of adult-to-juvenile ratio.

morning. The animal noises are there, but the people noises aren't and it is much quieter. So, if you happen to be coming in from an all-night party some fine May or June morning about daybreak, and if you should see a fellow standing by the road gazing around at the sky, with a watch in one hand and a clicker-counter in the other—and if you ask him if all is okay and he just stares past you without answering—he isn't necessarily rattle-brained, he may just be out there listening for doves. Which, if he *did* tell you, might sound rattle-brained, too, if you hadn't read this book.

Kill Surveys: Many of you are used to having a man "check your doves" in the field. For many years this was the main method of determining kill success, as well as the condition of the doves bagged. Note was also taken of whether the adult doves might be nesting and of the availability and preference of food materials. This checking was an important segment of the early life-history and management studies. More recently states have, while continuing some form of field bag checks for wing examination, potential breeders and such, shifted the estimating of the kill to the computer services. Present kill data are obtained by telephone surveys. Using long-distance wide-area telephone service (WATS), a random selection of numbers is called in each state within a Management Unit. The caller asks whether there is a dove hunter in the household. If so it is then determined how many doves he bagged. These statistics are expanded to fit the entire dove-hunting area in the state and then the entire Management Unit. This is one of those computer procedures where the data, lots of numbers, are cranked into a prepared program and the results are determined to be accurate within a given percentage or margin — with a measurable amount of confidence. The use of computers gives a great boost to wildlife management, because in this complex work a large part of the final results must be based on indefinite totals and there are also many variables and unknown factors that can affect the statistical picture of the game being studied.

Quite possibly, if you live east of the Mississippi river, where phone surveys have been conducted for the past several years, you may have been called. Or you may be called in the future. Or you may know someone who has been called. This is just one of many ways in which sportsmen are involved in the management of their game.

Wing Collections: The wing collections and examinations usually have been made by biologists in the field where the shooting takes place. Or, in some cases, envelopes are mailed out to hunters before the season opens. Each hunter who receives such envelopes is asked to send back all or a sample of wings from the doves he bags. This is to determine the ratio of young to old doves in the hunted populations. The annual population turnover and production periods and nesting peaks are assessed by studying the wings. A high percentage of young to adult doves would tend to reflect a successful nesting season. In doves this would mean about six or seven young to three or four adults. Other information on the hunt may be taken down by field biologists or, when the wings are to be mailed in, the questions can be printed

Biologist attaches aluminum band to leg of dove in study of population shifts and seasonal migration.

on the envelope that the hunter receives.

Banding and Marking: Dove banding is fascinating work, if you're not in too great a hurry for results. Once the band is attached, there is an always unpredictable time lapse before any information is received on the subsequent movement of the bird. Sometimes you hear about it right away, as you might expect when birds are banded just ahead of an open season. But sometimes—more often, in fact—you never hear of the bird again. It takes thousands of birds banded before you receive enough band returns to tell the story of movements of a group or species of birds. Three bands recovered out of 100 birds banded is what you might expect on the average. In certain cases, such as banding near a shooting area or giving the banding work some publicity, the band return increases. Yet I don't recall any recovery rate greater than 10 percent, and this would be rare even in a local area.

Banding is essential if we are to learn about a species of migratory bird. Banding (or ringing, as it's called in some countries) is of necessity controlled by the federal government when the birds being investigated are migratory. You can easily see the reason for this, with all the birds moving across state lines and even the country's borders. A federal and state banding permit must be obtained before a person can legally trap and band wild birds. This, too, is necessary to protect the birds and insure accurate records.

Dove bands are usually made of aluminum. They are furnished, along with record forms, to the permittee (bander) by the U.S. Fish and Wildlife Service. The size for doves is 3-A. This designates the number 3 band size, modified somewhat for a better fit on the adult dove leg. The bands are all stamped with a number and a return address. These are for record-keeping.

The bander attaches a band to a dove's leg, using a pair of banding pliers, and he records the date and location and pertinent information about the bird itself, such as whether it's a young bird,

After recovering banded dove in trap, biologist records vital statistics such as age and locale.

whether it's in apparent good health and any other special information needed. These are all listed in code on a banding schedule—a special sheet for recording bandings.

Periodically, normally every month with game birds, the schedules are mailed in to the Bird Banding Office in Washington, D.C., where the banding data are fed into the computers and are available for future study. Analyses of banding data will be continued indefinitely. The more we can

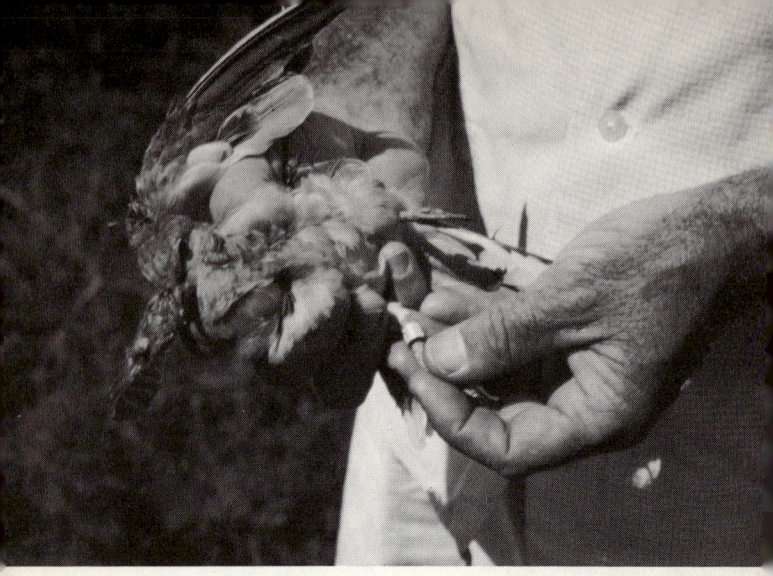

Hunter who downs banded dove can help management studies by mailing band to address stamped on it.

find out about dove movements, the better provisions can be made for looking after them. Tracing movements of populations over a Management Unit, within state boundaries, and conceivably on down to local production and harvest areas would be desirable.

Band recovery is a crucial problem. If a hunter shoots a dove with a band on its leg (this is not illegal as some hunters used to think) discarding the band or losing it defeats the efforts of game biologists. If, on the other hand, the hunter simply mails the band to the address stamped on it, he has helped to complete an important investigation—in effect writing the end of the story of that particular bird. He should list the date and the place where the dove was shot (or where it was found dead). And he should include his name and address if he wants to know about the bird's history. The hunter or the person who sends in the band, or both if their names are listed, will receive a report showing where the dove was banded and other information of interest to him. If the hunter wishes to keep the band for a souvenir he can ask that it be sent back to him.

Dove banding and the subsequent recapture of the bird or recovery of the band—as a result of shooting the dove, finding it dead or whatever—is of the highest importance in dove management work. This will be so until a lot more is revealed about dove migration and movements.

It may seem that a single band can't tell us much, but single bands add up to a banding program that tells a great deal. Of course, how much we learn depends in part on how many people cooperate by sending in those single bands. Every one counts. When a dove is banded, this starts a record or life story of that dove. Any time the dove is recaptured by trapping, the information is added to the story. When the band is taken from a dead dove, that completes the story. Many doves contribute many stories. Lots of the stories are the same, and these form patterns, revealing general movements, migration times and places and any

206 · *The Dove Shooter's Handbook*

Biologist takes mourning dove from trap. He will record relevant data, then band and release bird.

number of items of interest. Over a period of years of banding and recoveries, many thousands of stories are completed and we have greater knowledge to apply to the overall management picture.

So, whether a hunter sends in the band he takes off a dove or keeps it on his key chain or ignores it altogether has an effect on the banding program. You can help greatly by sending in any band you recover, and if another hunter kills a banded dove and asks about that little anklet, you can at least tell him why it was put there.

Marking doves with dyes of various colors has also been done in several states. Red, purple,

Doves have been removed from row of traps and bait has been replenished during continuing game study.

blue and green have been used, and in Florida the hunters were alerted by a story of their "flying oranges." Dyeing of the wing feathers was successful, as many observations were reported. Still, the band is the best because the reports are verified with the actual band.

The traps used for capture and recapture in banding projects mostly are made up of chicken wire, or poultry netting as it is sometimes called, with a heavy wire or wood frame. Some have trap doors and some have entrance funnels. Some are square and others are shaped like a clover leaf. They're made or modified to suit the trapper, and all of these variations have proved successful.

You may be wondering about "mist nets," which have been mentioned in books and quite a few magazine articles in connection with the study and management of game birds. Mist nets have been tried with doves and they do work, but are not as effective as the wire traps. They're more difficult to set up and more devilish to take doves out of. Mist nets are more often used on night-moving birds such as the woodcock.

A cannon-net trap has also seen some use. To set up this type of trap, projectiles are tied to ropes and attached to netting. When fired from mortar-type tubes, the projectiles pull the netting over doves that have been attracted to the bait. This type of trap has been successful but not as good as the wire traps. A wire trap can go untended and catch doves, whereas a cannon-net trap requires a man and a blind. The wire traps can be placed and replaced readily, anywhere in the field. But a cannon trap must go over a specific baited area. Finally, you can catch as many birds in one small wire trap—each time you run the trap—as you could expect to shoot a net over.

Banders have tried many designs for traps, depending on species and circumstances. Most of them are successful, but all bird banding requires work and certainly very accurate record-keeping. It is therefore not recommended as a mere hobby.

Habitat Studies: Dove nests have been found in all 48 contiguous states, and from sea level to elevations of some 10,000 feet or so. The birds use just about everything or anything that will provide a platform to build on. Space hardly seems a factor in nesting. Doves are so versatile in their choice that, in spite of the large nesting territories each pair seems to prefer, there is no apparent shortage of nest space. However, concern has been voiced by some workers in the Southwest and in prairie country where trees are scarce. In the Southwest certain plant-eradication programs have caused fear for the loss of possible nesting space; I think the main concern was for the white-winged dove in that area. In the prairie country the planting of shelterbelt trees has been recommended as a means of aiding dove nesting. Elsewhere, too, it could be very beneficial to plant long rows of trees for dove nest sites. This is certainly one possible management procedure that can be started anywhere and any time that people feel their dove population could or should be helped.

The question of nest support is more controversial. The flimsiness of the typical dove nest is a definite factor in ultimate breeding success, but it can't be assumed that sturdier structures such as baskets and other types of platforms would result

Artificial nesting structures are not necessary to maintain dove population, but doves will use them.

in a greater total of young produced. There's reason to suspect that the success of nesting platforms reduces the number of nestings, so the expected result wouldn't seem worth the effort as long as doves are faring reasonably well or where more can be achieved through habitat improvement like shelterbelt plantings and food plantings. Still, there's no harm done, and it's fun to see a dove come in and build its nest on a structure you put up for it.

Where special aid is deemed necessary or desirable, platforms or baskets or tarpaper cones

Dove incubates her clutch in simple nesting basket securely wired to tree by bird-watching sportsman.

can be placed to encourage an increase in the local population. Artificial measures have been used in many instances with other species and proved successful in raising local population levels. Not with doves, that I know of, but with other species. These artificial measures have not been tried on any large scale because they have not been regarded as necessary. The knowledge is there if and when someone determines that the population needs an assist.

Ideal Habitat: There do seem to be ideal year-round habitat components. While these are not required, they might make things a little easier and more desirable for doves. Obviously, habitat that makes the birds happier will attract and hold more of them. I was asked once to suggest ideal conditions for doves on a 40-acre area. I submitted the following:

1. Cropland; cereal-feed grains; no fall plowing: *20 acres*
2. Pasture; to include a pond (food-and-water in combination): *8 acres*
3. Deciduous woodlot (mast-nest-rest-shelter): *8 acres*
4. Random conifer (nest-shelter): *1 acre*
5. Natural stream and streambank (water-gravel-nest-rest): *2 acres*
6. Food plots; small grain; average ¼-acre per 10 acres: *1 acre*

Managed Food Plantings: Food plots, say, of millets and grain sorghums are put in for doves in some areas, but this is mostly to attract doves and hold them during the hunting season. Doves, of course, feed on these fields before and after the season, too, as do other game and non-game birds, so it is felt that overall benefits greatly exceed whatever losses to shooting may occur. While food plots may not be necessary to maintain present dove populations, planting is a handy tool that can

Field with widely spaced rows of brown-top millet is likely to attract doves during hunting season.

readily be instituted when and where it may be needed.

Some states have begun this managing of fields on state-owned lands for dove shooting where hunters have too little free access to private land for hunting. In other words, the fields are managed in order to create dove shooting for those who have no place to hunt—for public hunting. It would not be at all surprising to see more and more of this as cities grow bigger, so-called baby farms become more numerous, the few unprincipled hunters anger more landowners, and more landowners look on the granting of hunting privileges as a cash-crop opportunity.

Managed Hunters: From managing shooting fields, the next step is managing the hunters themselves—checking them in and out of areas, designating shooting stands, limiting access, limiting shells. Where the demand for shooting exceeds the available hunting space, all these things can and do come about. What started as a favor by game agencies, to make things easier for their dove shooters, might very well end up with a demand for more. Another thing to look for then would be the entrance of private individuals into the managed dove-hunting business for profit.

Behavior Studies

Findings and practices with regard to conditioning, or "imprinting" as it is called, may have considerable bearing on ground- and tree-nesting doves. (As mentioned in Chapter 2, ground-nesting is relatively uncommon, but doves sometimes set up housekeeping in seemingly odd places.) It appears that when a bird is hatched and very shortly afterwards, what the nestling observes is strongly and permanently imprinted into its behavior pattern. Its entire life is thus influenced. For example, if it first recognizes itself to be in a nest in a tree, then when it becomes ready to nest it will instinctively look for a tree of like size and dimensions and possibly even contour or other details of resemblance to the place of its hatching.

In this way, where trees are plentiful the doves are imprinted to be tree nesters. In less forested areas, ground nests would tend to be more common, and this surely is the case as ground nesting actually is more prevalent where trees are scarce. The same principle of instinct should apply to density. If suitable nesting habitat were in short supply and the young were hatched in relatively close-spaced nests, a dove produced there would in turn look among other nests to find a place for its own.

Carrying this a step further, it would be entirely logical for a student of bird behavior to design the habitat and produce a colony of doves that would search for platforms or baskets or other man-made nest accommodations. Controlled-behavior procedures have very interesting possibilities and could have very important application where new or more intensive habitat occupancy might be desired.

As we learn more about behavior and adaptability of our wild game species, the seemingly useless, pure-research experiments and investigations might be developed into management procedures. If needed, these controlled influences could provide the changes and adaptation to increase production and assure preservation of the species. When you stop to think about it, this is not greatly unusual. Wild animals from all over the world are being brought into zoos and adapting to artificial environments or conditions other than those natural to their places of origin. And the domestication of our turkeys, goats, cows, etc., was the adapting of these animals to conditions more beneficial to man. Hundreds of animals and plants have been cultivated to prosper through changes in environment, adapting to other than their natural conditions so that they could be utilized more conveniently or in greater numbers by man.

In most cases, studies of animal behavior require considerable operator time and often a lot of special equipment that can be expensive. They are therefore best suited to be worked out in the universities, where the operator may be a student working under expert supervision toward advanced degrees and where long-range studies can be continued year after year without a demand for quick, practical results.

Mortality Studies

Shooting: Hunter kill is a mortality factor to consider in all management studies. Though hunting has been given a section of its own, let me emphasize a few facts here. In my studies, the annual population turnover each year for the past 20 years or so has been recorded from 60 percent to 80 percent, varying slightly from one year to the next. It has not been established that hunting is accountable for more than perhaps 50 to 60 percent of the annual population, thus leaving a mortality of 20 to 30 percent due to other causes, including unknown factors. Hunting is not as selective of misfits as are natural losses, and it does take a toll. However, if losses due to natural causes were excessive enough to carry the broodstock below the estimated required level for the next year's normal production, shooting could be curtailed so as to provide every possible chance of survival to individual doves.

In times of deficit populations, all methods, however good or mediocre, proven or unproven, would be instituted to aid in rapid recovery to normal population levels. This is why dove shooting was curtailed in the East after the hard freeze and epidemic of trichomoniasis back in 1950–51. The population was known to be down from normal after the hard winter, so the hunting take was reduced to save all birds possible for the next spring's nesting season. Evidently this did some good. It is a management procedure always at hand, for use whenever needed.

Losses to Predators: The study of dove losses to predators is important so that in the event of serious population losses all controls could be instituted. Predator loss would almost have to be a local factor and local remedies applied. Outside of shooting, all losses are natural and tend to be compensated. Bountiful Mother Nature allows a surplus to be produced but then turns right around and wields the decimating factors—which include all the various predatory species that may be present in a dove region and would normally prey on birds.

The highest losses occur, as might be expected, during the nesting period, and the weak and unwitting go first. It has been noted in some non-hunting states that whether or not doves are shot, there will *still* be the 60 to 80 percent loss due to all causes from one year to the next. So current observations indicate that predators, including man, do not appear to be excessively harmful. Rather, they might in the long run be considered beneficial population-control factors. This means that no measures are presently needed to reduce predation, but if the situation changed then the

Dove Management · 219

emphasis of any control program would involve the nesting period since it is known that the highest losses occur then.

Food and Water Scarcity: Studies indicate that food or water scarcity is generally not a problem for doves. Even though they do not scratch, doves always find enough seeds to get by. Mobility is the key. Doves can move great distances when necessary to get sustenance. Pickings get slim during iced-over periods or in deep snow or in times of drought. But doves soon find the places where farmers are feeding and watering livestock, and they discover how to get under or into storage bins, lofts and water tanks. In the South, where the bulk of the migrants end up each winter, hard freezes don't usually last long. Doves find shelter and pickings in the woods and thickets during the short cold spells.

I don't recall any instance when a source of food or water had to be provided purely for the welfare of the doves. In connection with shooting, yes—food and water, provided in any area where such supplies are short, will surely concentrate flocks of doves. While such provision is now carried on primarily to benefit the shooter, it *could* be done as a highly beneficial management practice where and when needed. Enough is known of dove requirements to give them what they need in suitable habitat. Quite possibly these artificial methods could be used to help extend the range of doves into sparsely occupied areas.

Pesticides: Though pesticides are known killers of wildlife, doves seem to have a way of escaping the effects of these chemicals, possibly through their eating habits and also apparently through a certain tolerance for poisons. Two experiments I am aware of showed the dove to have a greater tolerance for certain poisons than the bobwhite quail. In another study of nesting doves in a commercial peach orchard, where many and frequent sprays are used, the dove nest success was about what would be expected for an unsprayed area. Still, we know that such pesticides do kill doves in certain concentrations as it has been demonstrated in controlled experiments. There is no practical way to prevent doves in the wild from taking in poisons where they are available. Any die-off where poison is suspected would be treated like any other population loss until more information could be gathered. If it were serious enough, hunting would be curtailed to protect the survivors for the nesting season.

Effects of Disease: Managing wild, free-moving populations of doves to include the control of diseases would not be practical. But it isn't omitted entirely. Most infective organisms and their effects are known or can probably be quickly isolated and recognized. Detailed studies have been made of the organisms that infect doves. A serious spread of disease, causing major losses in the overall population, would be treated the same as any other population reduction factor. The first thing—the easiest thing—to do would be to curtail hunting to give protection to the survivors. When a disease hits, it soon runs its course, and in a year or so things are back to normal or are getting back to normal.

Weather: Management studies with regard to the weather are much like those of disease and pesticides. We learn about it and how to recognize the danger signs and how to evaluate the serious effects. When it is bad enough to cause large losses to the population, the same hunting-control measures can be instituted. (It's safe to say that the hunter pays for wildlife conservation not only in terms of money but in the way his outdoor activities are governed.) I don't know of any losses due to weather alone that caused an altering of hunting seasons. In the Southeast, weather and disease together, in the winter of 1950–51, brought the most serious losses that I am aware of, at least in the past 25 years. This was a particularly hard double-barreled clout that cut deep into the population totals. Hunting was drastically reduced and population levels were watched closely until the population was back to normal. Weather is known to be rough on doves during the early part of the nesting season; at that time of year the warm spells start doves nesting, then the cold, windy rain squalls and storms destroy the nests. But these setbacks are to be expected and so far as I know they have no effect on the total annual production.

Regulations and Prime Future Needs

The regulation of our shooting privileges is the most important single management tool in use today. Laws and their enforcement are the final putting into practice of the rules devised from studies of population levels and factors affecting them. Laws are made to insure that both the hunter and the game get a fair shake. Several study jobs are carried on at all times and the results lead to decisions that guide the setting of regulations.

Each year's dove population is a separate entity—like a corn crop. Though you use the same type of seed each year, the success of production depends on a particular year's environmental circumstances and does not necessarily have to be as it was the year before or the year after. The yearly data are prepared for study and discussion. Where enough signs indicate that a change may be needed, the change is proposed, discussed, adopted or rejected by the regulations committee. For example, laws governing shooting areas, baiting, agricultural practices and early and late shooting were tested in the field and the results then studied. The final action was to change the rules, in some cases to benefit the dove and in some cases to benefit the hunter.

Some states may prefer split seasons or zoning so as to allow greater hunter opportunity without taking too great a portion of the doves. These changes provide for more timely and equitable dove harvest in all parts of the state. It is not unusual for a state or group of states to be more restrictive with the shooting privileges than the federal hunting regulations would allow; thus, working within the federal framework, a region can give the dove more protection when more protection is needed.

While we have racked up an impressive number of studies and results, there still are confusing blanks in our knowledge of population peaks, movements and hunter kill. I expect that the investigation of these blanks will be where management emphasis is placed in the future. Then, as more is learned, the regulations may be modified accordingly.

To be put into final draft form are the findings of a five-year study of the effect of shooting on population levels in the Eastern Management Unit. The results of the study should provide a long look into the future as to where and what other studies should now be initiated. This study, incidentally, was one of the prime "National Mourning Dove Management Needs," as determined by the Bureau of Sport Fisheries and Wildlife and the International Association of Game and Fish Commissioners and reported in the fall of 1960.

The three prime needs mentioned at that time were:
1. To ascertain whether and how hunting affects the total population.
2. To improve methods and devise new methods to count or measure populations.
3. To relate nesting areas to shooting areas; that is to find out exactly what state and location produce the doves you shoot.

The International Association of Game and Fish Commissioners took a step to emphasize these studies by arranging to have a discussion of the progress of national dove programs at their annual regulations meeting. In March of 1961, the Bureau of Sport Fisheries and Wildlife published *The Mourning Dove Program For the Future*. This included acknowledgment of the need for dove research, a presentation of the management goals (stated essentially as above) and the program for their development.

In some areas of the West, wildlife-management personnel are greatly concerned over the depletion of whitewing-dove habitat. The mourning-dove population, on the other hand, has prospered and extended its range in some areas.

Management, including regulations, does not deal with forces or practices aimed at increasing overall mourning-dove production, at least for now. The dove has demonstrated that it can pretty well take care of itself if given the chance. The dove is a multi-brooded species—our only game bird that may have several broods in a year—so the loss of two or perhaps even three broods in one season would not be disastrous. Food, water, nesting sites and other environmental requirements are apparently ample and in some instances appear to be improving due to changes in land use. This species is not in any danger—except perhaps as man endangers his own survival.

7
Questions and Prospects

I've been asked where and when the hunting is best; how a man who's more accustomed to other game can plan a trip and find good shooting; whether doves are extending their range and increasing their numbers and—perhaps most important—whether future prospects look bright for doves and dove shooters. To anyone looking for good wingshooting sport those questions may seem crucial, but the answers aren't cut and dried. I'll do my best to cover each point in this final chapter.

An inevitable question is, "Where's the best dove shooting? Alabama? Missouri? Arizona?" And I have to say, yes. And also in Florida, Texas, California. . . . Doves are migratory, and so dove shooting is where you find them, literally. Once you see a flock of doves and locate their feeding grounds, the shooting is best right there, no matter

Shooter adds dove to his bag during typically productive recent season. Birds appear to be prospering.

what state or region you are in. For example, you might go out one day in Mississippi and shoot one box of shells and get your limit in two hours, or you might hunt in New Mexico and shoot two boxes of shells and get your limit of birds in one hour. Where was the best shooting? I'd say in both places, wouldn't you? As I see it, the best shooting and the best time to go can be summed up as anywhere you can get to as often as you can.

I'm sure many readers, especially those who might have to do some traveling to reach a dove-hunting state, would like me to go farther out on a limb concerning the when and where. As far as I'll go is to suggest a few things to keep in mind if you are new at dove hunting: The earlier in the season you go, the better. Up until about the end of September, doves remain largely in their nesting range. At this time, *any* state that has an open season is going to have some good shooting. After October 1, your chances are best in the South, regardless of which Management Unit you are in.

One sure way to pinpoint the better shooting dates is to note the *opening* dates — be there then! Each state's game-management people have their own population levels pegged and arrange their seasons to give hunters the best opportunity.

If you live in a state where dove hunting is permitted, ask around. Someone you know will be able to get you started. And write to your state's game agency—to the Director, Division of Game Management, Fish and Wildlife Department, State Capital. Ask about dove shooting, and even if your state doesn't allow dove shooting the game division can suggest where else to write for information and hunting details in your region or the nearest region. You can also get a copy of the federal regulations, look up the states with seasons and write to their game agencies for advice on hunting there, on travel, hunting clubs, lands open to hunters, accommodations, etc.

You'll note in the regulations that some states allow all-day shooting, while others open only from noon to sunset. Regardless of where you shoot, you'll have to comply with both state and federal regulations. You'll also note that the regulations specify current possession limits as well as bag limits. For example, the daily bag limit may be 12 and the possession limit 24. That means you can have no more than 24 doves in your possession at any time. If you go on a dove-shooting trip and hunt for three days where there's a daily limit of 12 you can legally shoot only two dozen in that time —unless you give away or eat 12 of them—since you may possess or transport only the possession limit of 24 (or whatever the limit is where you hunt). Another caution: When transporting your game, you must have the head or one wing attached to each dove so that a wildlife officer can identify the bird. That, too, is in the game regulations.

Incidentally, while I'm on the subject of transporting doves, let me mention that I've found it's better to carry them refrigerated, rather than frozen. Usually it's no problem to keep birds iced down during travel but it's more difficult to keep them frozen. The meat certainly isn't improved if you freeze it and then it thaws and you have to refreeze it. So I'd suggest that you keep your doves refrigerated or at least cool until you get home, then—if you wish to keep them longer—put them in the freezer.

Now here's an instant replay of the main points about planning a dove hunt: Write to your game department for information; go early and go by the rules; and in most cases you're well advised to hunt your own state or states south of you.

A big, double-barreled question is whether doves are likely to extend their range and whether they're likely to increase in numbers. The answer has to be strictly speculative. Instead of making any arguable predictions, I'd rather just discuss it and let you draw your own conclusions.

The whitewing remains a Southwestern game bird but the mourning dove is now found throughout the U.S. and has proved to be very adaptable to changing conditions. It appears to have prospered with the changes in agricultural methods and with the human population expansion and all that goes with that. I'd expect that doves would move in wherever more timber lands are cleared and more grain is grown, more area converted to agriculture and industry and the resulting towns with their trees and shrubs and landscaping and so on. This, I feel sure, would take place in the Eastern Management Unit with which I am most familiar.

The Central and Western Management Units have the great forested areas but also vast open spaces. Doves prefer edge-type habitat. More agriculture and more clearing of large timber tracts in the lower elevations might improve dove habitat with the increase of farm-woodland border. On the other hand, the clearing of scattered patches of woodland growth, regardless of size, amid miles and miles of open country, would *reduce* the edge effect and with it the doves' habitat.

There is no pat answer as to the future of doves in this type of country. It is a good subject for prolonged and detailed study. Managing habitat for doves, specifically to increase production, is an available tool. I don't know of its being used except experimentally, but it could be most important in future game-management programs.

In discussing the prospects, perhaps there should be some mention of what kind of changes in dove *hunting* might come about. For one thing, it is becoming a more managed sport. The dove supply is managed by the shooting rules, while dove shooting is getting more and more attention from the hunting clubs and hunting farms and private farms that cater to shooters. More and more groups of hunters are getting together and renting farmland for the sake of exclusive hunting privileges, too. These practices are common for the hunting of species such as deer and waterfowl, and the same trend is becoming more pronounced in dove shooting, especially around the urban areas in the more southern states. Another trend with much the same purpose and results is that of the farmer who opens his lands to dove shooters for a head-fee—everybody's welcome at so much per person for the day's shooting.

Less discussed but also expanding is the use of such fees as a means to raise funds for charities. For example, a farmer will charge so much per person to shoot over his fields and will turn the money over to his church. Another practice that's becoming more prevalent is the renting of a dove-shooting field by a manufacturing company or some other business for the purpose of entertaining clients or customers or otherwise promoting sales. It's the same sort of promotion as the giving away of season tickets to ball games for business purposes. The whirlwind nature of dove shooting lends itself nicely to such commercial ventures.

And what else may be expected for dove shooting? What about the years ahead? Judging by what I've seen, I expect dove shooting to become even more popular. I expect more states to have open seasons. There are, of course, active groups that oppose dove shooting. But with better understanding of dove-population dynamics, plus the growing realization that game-management agencies are not made up of killers, plus the recognition that present game-management programs are of great benefit to songbirds and other non-game species, much of the resistance will be withdrawn. Even those who oppose shooting must be impressed by the fact that many private outdoor clubs and similar organizations are now collecting their own funds and turning them over to state game agencies to offset the cost and promote better management of non-game species.

Finally, there's the question of how long the dove population can hold up under continually increasing hunting pressure. In preceding chapters I described how the dove is apparently holding its own and possibly increasing its numbers right

Proper conservation can assure this young gunner of doves when his shotgun is no longer too big for him.

along with the increase in shooting. Still, there has to be a limit and if the increase in shooters continues it would be logical to expect an eventual drop in the dove population. This is one of the main reasons for population studies and annual inventory checks and production estimates—to keep abreast of the population trends and adjust game harvests accordingly. As soon as any significant drop is noticed, you'll know about it from changes in the regulations. The bag limit, opening dates and length of season—one or all would be modified accordingly. And you may be sure of adequate enforcement.

The evolutionary changes in dove hunting are not necessarily bad. There will be more states with open seasons, there will be more shooters and there will be more private funds devoted to dove management. And there will be even more attention given to fluctuations in the dove population and to their protection. My conclusion from those trends? I'd say the future of dove hunting looks just great. You're likely to have a lot of shooting. Good luck!

Thoughtful shooter looks back across land and water that produce wildlife harvest as well as agricultural crops.

Selected Bibliography of Dove Literature

Aldrich, John W. 1956. *Migration of Breeding Populations of Mourning Doves Determined from Races Identified in Hunters' Bags in Texas and Georgia.* Mourning Dove Newsletter No. 11. U.S.D.I. Fish and Wildlife Service.

Alexander, Harold E. 1951. *Mourning Dove Study.* Final Report, Project 24-R. Arkansas Game and Fish Commission.

Allen, John M. 1963. *Primary Feather Molt Rate of Wild Immature Doves in Indiana.* Indiana Department of Conservation, Division of Fish and Game. Circular Number 4. 7 pp.

Allison, Don. 1951. *Mourning Dove Study.* Project 30-R. North Carolina Wildlife Resources Commission.

Arnold, Lee W. 1943. *The White-Winged Dove in Arizona.* Pittman-Robertson Project 9-R. 103 pp.

Austin, Oliver L., Jr. 1951. *The Mourning Dove on Cape Cod.* Bird Banding 22 (4): 149–174.

Bobbs, Henry, Jr. 1952. *Mourning Dove Study.* Final Report. Project 25-R-3. Mississippi Game and Fish Commission.

Bobbs, Henry, Jr. 1952. *The Mourning Dove and Cotton Dusting in the Mississippi Delta.* Report of the Mississippi Game and Fish Commission.

Boldt, Wilbur and George O. Hendrickson. 1952. *Mourning Dove Production in North Dakota Shelterbelts.* Journal of Wildlife Management 16: 187–191.

Calhoun, John B. 1948. *Utilization of Artificial Nesting Substrate by Doves and Robins.* Journal of Wildlife Management 12 (2): 136.

Cole, F. J. 1933. *The Relation of Light Periodicity to the Reproduction Cycle, Migration and Distribution of the Mourning Dove.* Auk 50: 284–296.

Cottam, Clarence and James B. Trefethen. 1968. *Whitewings: The Life History, Status and Management of the White-Winged Dove.* Van Nostrand.

Cowan, John B. 1952. *Life History and Productivity of a Population of Western Mourning Doves in California.* California Fish and Game 38 (4): 505–521.

Dahlen, James H. 1951. *The Effect of Certain Insecticides on the Bobwhite Quail and Mourning Dove.* Transactions, Fifth Annual Conference, Southeastern Association of Game and Fish Commissioners.

Dahlgren, Robert B. 1955. *Factors Affecting Mourning Dove Populations in Utah.* Progress Report. Utah Wildlife Cooperative Research Unit.

Dalrymple, Byron W. 1949. *Doves and Dove Shooting*. G. P. Putnam's Sons.

Downing, Robert L. 1956. *An Analysis of Ground Nesting by Mourning Doves in Northwestern Oklahoma*. Progress Report. Oklahoma A&M College.

Fichter, Edson. 1956. *Mourning Dove Production in Southeastern Idaho*. Manuscript typed, 11 pp.

Foote, Leonard E. 1957. *Suggestions for a Mourning Dove Management Plan*. Manuscript processed, 14 pp.

Foote, Leonard E. 1960. *National Mourning Dove Program Needs, Responsibilities and Implementation*. Dove Committee Report. Fourteenth Annual Conference, Southeastern Association of Game and Fish Commissioners. Mimeo 4 pp.

Gallizioli, Steve. 1961. *Present Status and Management of the Mourning Dove in the Western Management Unit*. Transactions, Twenty-Sixth North American Wildlife and Natural Resources Conference.

Ginn, William E. 1951. *Status of the Eastern Mourning Dove in Indiana*. Thirteenth Midwest Wildlife Conference. Mimeo 2 pp.

Goforth, Reid W. 1971. *The Three-Bird Chase in Mourning Doves*. The Wilson Bulletin 83 (4):

419–424.

Graefe, C. F. and U. F. Hollander. 1945. *A Pale Mutant Mourning Dove*. The Auk 62:300.

Hammond, James W. 1956. *The Mourning Dove in Tennessee*. Final Report Project W-11-R. Tennessee Game and Fish Commission.

Hanson, H. C. and C. W. Kossack. 1957. *Methods and Criteria for Aging Incubated Eggs and Nestlings of the Mourning Dove*. The Wilson Bulletin 69 (1): 91–101.

Haugen, Arnold O. 1952. *Trichomoniasis in Alabama Mourning Doves*. Journal of Wildlife Management 16:164–169.

Haugen, Arnold O. and James E. Keeler. 1952. *Mortality of Mourning Doves from Trichomoniasis in Alabama during 1951*. Transactions, Seventeenth North American Wildlife Conference.

Harris, S. W. 1961. *Migrational Homing in Mourning Doves*. Journal of Wildlife Management 25 (1):61–65.

Hayne, Don W. 1967. *Mourning Dove Banding Information, Eastern Management Unit, 1965–1966*. Institute of Statistics, North Carolina State University. Mimeo 10 pp.

Hayne, Don W. 1968. *Call Count Route Information Summarized for the Eastern Management Unit, 1960–1967*. Institute of Statistics, North Carolina State University. Mimeo 56 pp.

Herman, Carleton M. 1950. *Trichomoniasis, a Disease of Mourning Doves.* U.S.D.I. Fish and Wildlife Service. Leaflet Number 331.

Howarth, Robert C. 1954. *A Study of Migration and Nesting of the Mourning Dove in Center County, Pennsylvania.* M.Sc. Thesis, Pennsylvania State University.

Jenkins, James H. 1960. *The Technique for Aging and Sexing Doves throughout the Shooting Season in the Eastern United States.* Dove Committee Report. Fourteenth Annual Conference, Southeastern Association of Game and Fish Commissioners. Mimeo 7 pp.

Kaczynski, C. F. and W. H. Kiel, Jr. 1960. *Band Loss in Nestling Mourning Doves.* Dove Committee Report. Fourteenth Annual Conference, Southeastern Association of Game and Fish Commissioners. Mimeo 17 pp.

Keeler, James E. and Frank W. Winston. 1951. *Mourning Dove Trapping in the Southeast.* Bird Banding 22 (4):174–179.

Keeler, James E. 1952. *The Mourning Dove Study.* Final Report, Project 22-R. Alabama Department of Conservation.

Kerley, Clayton. 1952. *The Call-Road Count as an Index to Breeding Populations of the*

Mourning Dove in East Tennessee. U.S.D.I. Fish and Wildlife Service, Special Scientific Report Number 17.

Kiel, W. H., Jr. 1959. *Mourning Dove Management Units—a Progress Report.* U.S.D.I. Fish and Wildlife Service, Special Scientific Report Number 42.

Kiel, W. H., Jr. 1960. *Banding Analysis and Needs—a Report to the Southeastern Dove Committee.* Dove Committee Report. Fourteenth Annual Conference, Southeastern Association of Game and Fish Commissioners. Mimeo 2 pp.

Kossack, Charles W. and Harold Hanson. 1953. *Unisexual Broods of the Mourning Dove.* Journal of Wildlife Management 17 (4):541.

Laub, Kenneth W. 1956. *The Relation of Parental Care and the Condition of the Glandular Crop to the Successful Rearing of Young Mourning Doves, Zenaidura Macroura* (L). M.Sc. Thesis, Ohio State University.

Lincoln, Frederick C. 1945. *The Mourning Dove as a Game Bird.* U.S.D.I. Fish and Wildlife Service, Circular 10.

Locke, Louis N. and David H. Reese. 1960. *Trials of Two Methods for the Proposed Dove Disease Surveillance System.* Dove Committee Report. Fourteenth Annual Conference,

Southeastern Association of Game and Fish Commissioners. Mimeo 9 pp.

Mayer, U. V. *Observations on the Speed of the Mourning Dove.* Condor 45:38.

McClure, H. E. 1939. *Cooing Activity and Censusing of the Mourning Dove.* Journal of Wildlife Management 3:323–328.

McClure, H. E. 1942. *Mourning Dove Production in Southwestern Iowa.* The Auk 59:64–75.

McGowan, Terry A. 1953. *The Call Count as a Census Method for Breeding Mourning Doves in Georgia.* Journal of Wildlife Management 17 (4):437–445.

Moore, George C. 1940. *The Nesting Habits and Juvenile Development of the Mourning Dove in Alabama.* M.Sc. Thesis, Alabama Poly. Institute.

Moore, George C. and Allen M. Pearson. 1941. *The Mourning Dove in Alabama.* Bulletin. Alabama Department of Conservation.

Moore, George C., Harold S. Peters and Leonard E. Foote. 1953. *Progress Report of the Cooperative Dove Study, 1948–1952.*

Nelson, Arnold L. and Alexander C. Martin. 1953. *Gamebird Weights.* Journal of Wildlife Management 17 (1):36–42.

Nelson, Dan. 1952. *Mourning Dove Study in Georgia.* Final Report, Project 17-R. Georgia

Game and Fish Commission.

Nelson, Frank P. 1953. *The Mourning Dove Study in South Carolina.* Final Report, Project 11-R. South Carolina Wildlife Resources Department.

Newsom, John D., J. B. Kidd and Robert E. Murry. 1953. *Mourning Dove Management in Louisiana.* Louisiana Conservationist 5 (8):16–18.

Newsom, John D., Dan M. Russell, Frank A. Winston, Leonard E. Foote and Harold S. Peters. 1957. *A Summary of Mourning Dove Investigations, 1948–1956.* Transactions, Twenty-Second North American Wildlife Conference.

Pearson, Allen M. and George C. Moore, 1940. *Feathers May Reveal Age of Mourning Doves.* Alabama Conservationist. November, pp 9–10.

Peters, Harold S. 1951. *Analysis of Recent Recoveries of Banded Mourning Doves.* U.S.D.I. Fish and Wildlife Service. Processed 7 pp.

Peters, Harold S. 1956. *Banding—a Key to Dove Management.* Transactions, Twenty-First North American Wildlife Conference, pp. 365–375.

Quay, Thomas L. 1950. *Mourning Dove Studies in North Carolina, 1939–1942.* Final Report,

Projects 2-R and 26-R. North Carolina Wildlife Resources Commission.

Randall, Robert N. 1955. *Mourning Dove Production in South Central North Dakota*. Journal of Wildlife Management 19 (1):157–159.

Ruos, James L. 1972. *Mourning Dove Status Report, 1971*. U.S.D.I. Fish and Wildlife Service, Special Scientific Report Number 158.

Russell, Dan M. 1954. *Kentucky Mourning Dove Study*. Final Report, Project 25-R. Kentucky Department of Fish and Wildlife Resources.

Russell, Dan M. 1955. *Do We Really Shoot Migrant Doves?* Proceedings, Ninth Annual Southeastern Association of Game and Fish Commissioners Conference, October, 1955, pp 69–71.

Russell, Dan M. 1961. *Present Status and Management of the Mourning Dove in the Eastern Management Unit*. Transactions, Twenty-Sixth North American Wildlife and Natural Resources Conference.

Schultz, Vincent. 1951. *Game Mortality Resulting from a Severe Snow and Ice Storm in Tennessee*. Transactions, Fifth Annual Southeastern Association of Game and Fish Commissioners Conference.

Smith, Parker and William Davis. 1960. *Report on Effects of Changes in Dove Regulations*.

Dove Committee Report, Fourteenth Annual Southeastern Association of Game and Fish Commissioners Conference.

Southeastern Association of Game and Fish Commissioners. 1957. *Mourning Dove Investigations—1948–1956*. Technical Bulletin Number 1.

Stabler, Robert M. and Carleton M. Herman. 1951. *Upper Digestive Tract Trichomoniasis in Mourning Doves and Other Birds*. Transactions, Sixteenth North American Wildlife Conference, pp 146–163.

Stern, W. H. and Eugene Legler, Jr. 1960. *Investigations toward a Reliable Method for Estimating Dove Kill*. Proceedings, Fourteenth Annual Southeastern Association of Game and Fish Commissioners Conference.

Swank, Wendell G. 1950. *Dove Wings Yield Important Information*. Texas Game and Fish Commission. 8 (3) February, 1950.

Swank, Wendell G. 1952. *Contributions to the Knowledge of the Life History and Ecology of the Mourning Dove in Texas*. Ph.D. Thesis, Texas A&M College. May, 1952. 157 pp.

Wagner, Fred H. 1951. *Preliminary Investigations on Mourning Dove Index and Survey Methods in Wisconsin*. Thirteenth Midwest Wildlife Conference. December, 1951.

Mimeo 5 pp.

Webb, Lloyd G. 1950. *The Life History and Status of the Mourning Dove, Zenaidura macroura carolinensis (L.) in Ohio.* Ph.D. Thesis, Ohio State University.

Wight, Howard M. 1954. *Needed: A Dove Flyway Concept.* Proceedings, Eighth Annual Southeastern Game and Fish Commissioners Conference, November, 1954, pp. 78–79.

Wight, Howard M. 1956. *A Field Technique for Bursal Inspection of Mourning Doves.* Journal of Wildlife Management 20 (1):94–95.

Wight, Howard M. 1961. *Present Status and Management of the Mourning Dove in the Central Management Unit.* Transactions, Twenty-Sixth North American Wildlife and Natural Resources Conference.

Winston, Frank A. 1952. *Flying Oranges.* Florida Wildlife 6 (4):7, 8, 9, 50.

Winston, Frank A. 1953. *The Effect of Hunting on the Dove Population.* Transactions, Seventh Annual Southeastern Association of Game and Fish Commissioners Conference. Mimeo 11 pp.

Winston, Frank A. 1954. *Status, Movement and Management of the Mourning Dove in Florida.* Final Report, Project 22-R. Technical Bulletin Number 2. Florida Game and

Freshwater Fish Commission.

Young, Howard, Andrew Hulsey and Robert Moe. 1952. *Effects of Certain Cotton Insecticides on the Mourning Dove*. Proceedings, Arkansas Academy of Science, pp. 43–45.

Index

adaptability of wildlife to man-made habitats, 216
aging in doves, 20, 40–41
    feather characteristics indicating, 39, 40–42; tables of, 43, 166–67
albino doves, 35
Allen, John M., 42
altricial species, dove as an, 54, 60
American Ornithology (Bonaparte), 17
Audubon Society, 188

bag limits, 21, 97, 156, 157, 158–59, 229, 234
baiting regulations, 155, 156, 161, 223
banding, 20, 42, 79, 80, 201–6
band recovery, problem of, 204–6
barred dove, 152
behavior of hunters, offensive and objectionable, 30–31, 162, 170–73
behavior patterns of doves, 91–93,
    studies of, 214–16
bird watchers, value of, 189
Bonaparte, Prince Charles Lucien, 17

breeding doves, shooting of, 167–68

"cactus dove," 103
call counts, 195–98
calls, use of, in dove shooting, 128
camouflage, hunter's use of, 129
census of doves, recording and study of, 193–95
colonial nesting, 48, 215–16
coloration of doves, 33–35
conservation of natural resources, 26, 28–30, 96. *See also* management
cooing dove census, 195–98
cooking dove meat, 142–49
Cooking Over Coals by Mel Marshall, 144
coolness, importance of, in preserving dove meat, 139–40, 230
costs to hunter, dove-shooting, 22–25
courtship and mating, 51–52
crippling and loss of birds, 105, 119, 169

decoys, use of, in dove shooting, 128

Deep-Fried Doves, 145–46
diseases of doves, 82–85
  effects of, 220–21
dogs for retrieving shot doves, 130, 132–35
"dove milk," 55, 168
Doves Arkansas, 146
dressing doves for meat, 137, 138–42
Duck Stamp (Migratory Bird Hunting Stamp), 189

eating, shooting doves for, 22–25
economy, value of doves to, 175–77
eggs, laying and hatching of, 53, 54–55
eggshells, discarding of, 60–61
esthetic values in dove shooting, 112–16

feathers, molting of, 38–40
Federal Aid to Wildlife Restoration Fund, 25, 100, 174
Federal agencies for wildlife management, 181–84, 188–89
feeding habits, 66–68, 101, 102, 103
field dressing of shot doves, 137–39, 140–42
field position, hunter's, 123
Fisheries and Wildlife Bureau, *see* U.S. Bureau of Sport Fisheries and Wildlife
flocking habits of doves, 91, 125
food, occasional scarcity of, 129
food plantings, managed, 159, 212–14
foods, preferred, 66, 68–74
Foote, Leonard E., 191
fowl pox, 85
freezing, dove injuries caused by, 88–89
funds for wildlife management, sources of, 186–90, 233
future needs, study of, in dove management, 222–25

grit requirement, 75, 76
ground nesting, 48, 214–15
guns for dove shooting, 116, 120

habitat, 45–46, 67, 111, 214–16, 219, 231
  studies of, 209–12
  ideal, 211–12
head-fees, 232
How to Cook His Goose (and Other Wild Games) by Karen Green and Betty Black, 144
hunting, effect of, on dove population, 173–75. *See also* behavior of hunters

hunting clubs and farms, 232
hunting laws, *see* regulations and laws, hunting
hunting pressure, effects of, 123–25, 174, 233
hunting restrictions, *see* regulations and laws, hunting *and* restrictions, hunting
hunting success, 165–66

identifying doves in flight, 110–11
importance of dove as game bird, 18, 174–75
International Association of Game and Fish Commissioners, 224

Jenkins, James H., 42
jump-shooting, 130

kill surveys, 199–200

laceneck dove, 152
land use, effect of changes in, on doves, 20
Lincoln, Frederick C., 19, 46

management of doves, 21, 106
  defined, 179–81
  of food planting, 159, 212–14
  of hunters, 214, 232
  future needs in, study of, 222–25
  of habitat, experimental, 231–32
Management Units, 79, 97, 157, 158, 184, 199, 224, 231; map of, 182–83
Marinated Broiled Doves, 147
market hunting, 96. *See also* eating, shooting doves for
marking doves with dyes, 206–7
mating habits, *see* courtship and mating
melanism in doves, 35
Mexico-U.S. migratory bird treaty, 151
migration, 46, 47, 77–80, 151
Migratory Birds Treaty Act, 46, 96, 151, 155
"milk," *see* "dove milk"
"mist nets," 208
molting in doves, 38–40
Moore, George C., 191
mortality of doves, causes of, 20 nesting, 64. *See also* pesticides
mortality studies, 217–18. *See also* kill surveys
mourning dove (*Zenaida macroura macroura: Z. macroura carolinensis, Z. macroura marginella*), 17–18, 19–20
  coloration, 34
  distribution of, 47
  feeding habits of, 66–67
  shooting seasons on, 97–98

range of, 230–31
Mourning Dove Program for the Future, The, 224
multiple brood characteristic in doves, 65, 225

"National Mourning Dove Management Needs," 224
nest building and materials, 53–54
nesting, 46, 47, 214–16
  differences between mourning doves and whitewings, 48–49
  territory, 50–51
  period of, 52
  success in, average, 61–64
  mortality, 64–65
nests, artificial, 65, 209–11, 215–16

Outdoor Cook's Bible, The, by Joseph D. Bates, Jr., 144
Outdoor News Bulletin, 26

pass shooting, 101, 119, 125
passenger pigeons, 48, 96
parasites, 86–87
Patuxent Wildlife Research Station, 184
personnel in wildlife management, 185–86, 188
pesticides, danger to doves of, 77, 87–88, 220
Peters, Harold S., 190, 191

pigeon family *(Columbidae),* 18
polluters, hunters as, 30–31, 137, 170–71
popularity of dove hunting, 163–65, 233
population production peak, 80, 153, 200, 230
populations, dove, estimates of, 79, 80
  annual turnover in, 80–81, 200, 217
predators, losses to, 86, 106, 218
private agencies for wildlife management, 185, 188

rain, shooting in, 108–10

random road census of doves, 193;
  chart of, 194
range of doves in North America, 45–47, 230
regulations and laws, dove hunting, 21, 70, 96–97, 152–55, 157–62, 229
  practical effects of, 222–25
  potential changes in, 233–34
reproductive potential of doves, 65–66. *See also* courtship and mating
restrictions, hunting, 70, 155–56, 223
  on rifles, 162–63

retriever dogs, 130, 132–35
rifles, restrictions on use of, 162–63
rock dove (domestic pigeon), 18
Roast Doves with Grapes and Wine, 147
roost shooting, 105–6, 124

salt, doves' liking for, 76–77
Sautéed Doves with Chestnut-Mushroom Sauce, 148–49
seasonal movements of doves, 80.
 See also migration
seasons, dove-shooting, 152–53, 158, 228, 234
 split, 97, 223
shells and shot for dove shooting, 118–19, 120
shooting areas, 124–25, 130, 159, 223, 224, 227–28
shooting dates, *see* seasons
shooting over feed, 101–4
shooting techniques, 122
size and weight of doves, 33, 168–69
Southeastern States Cooperative Mourning Dove Investigations Study, 156, 191–93
speed characteristic in doves, 92–93, 110
split seasons, 97, 223
state agencies for wildlife management, 184, 186–87, 229
studies in dove management, 190–208
Swank, Wendell G., 42

trapping doves for banding, 207–8
trichomoniasis, 82–85, 218
Turtled Doves, 148

U.S. Bureau of Sport Fisheries and Wildlife, 19, 152, 195–96, 224

value to economy of doves, 175–76

walking them up, 129–30
"Wanton Waste" law, 156, 169
water-hole shooting, 108
water requirements of doves, 75–76, 91, 92
water, occasional scarcity of, 219
Waterman, Charles F., 130
weather, effect of, on doves, 88–91, 221–22
"webless migratory birds," 188–89
weight of doves, 33, 168–69
white-winged dove *(Zenaida asiatica)*, 18, 209
 size and color of, 35–38
 nesting range of, 46, 97, 230
 feeding habits of, 66

shooting seasons on, 97–98
flight style of, 105
wide-area telephone service (WATS), use of, in kill surveys, 199
Wildlife Federation, 188
wildlife management, *see* management
Wildlife Management Institute, 25–26, 188
Wildlife Restoration Act, Pittman-Robertson, 186–87
Wildlife Restoration Fund, 25, 100, 174
wing collection for census of doves, 200
writings on game birds, 18

young doves, parental care of, 54–55, 59–61

Zenaida dove, 17, 152
zoning, 223